GETTING THEM
TO GIVE A DAMN

HOW TO GET YOUR FRONT LINE
TO CARE ABOUT YOUR BOTTOM LINE

ERIC CHESTER

KAPLAN PUBLISHING

This publication is designed to provide accurate and authoritative information in regard to the subject matter covered. It is sold with the understanding that the publisher is not engaged in rendering legal, accounting, or other professional service. If legal advice or other expert assistance is required, the services of a competent professional person should be sought.

Vice President and Publisher: Cynthia A. Zigmund
Acquisitions Editor: Jonathan Malysiak
Senior Managing Editor: Jack Kiburz
Interior Design: Lucy Jenkins
Cover Design: Design Solutions
Typesetting: the dotted i

Published by Kaplan Publishing,
A division of Kaplan, Inc.

Printed in the United States of America

07 10 9 8 7 6 5

Library of Congress Cataloging-in-Publication Data

Chester, Eric.
    Getting them to give a damn : how to get your front line to care about your bottom line / by Eric Chester.
        p.   cm.
    Includes index.
    ISBN 1-4195-0458-4 (6x9 pbk.)
        1. Personnel management—United States.   2. Teenagers—Employment—United States.   3. Young adults—Employment—United States.
    4. Employee motivation—United States.   5. Employee retention—United States.   I. Title.
    HF5549.2.U5C44 2005
    658.3′14—dc22
                                                                    2004029168

For information about ordering Kaplan Publishing books at special quantity discounts, please call 1-800-KAP-ITEM or write to Kaplan Publishing, 888 Seventh Avenue, 22nd floor, New York, NY 10106.

PRAISE FOR *GETTING THEM TO GIVE A DAMN*

"Businesses need to stop focusing on 'paradigm shifts' and 'strategic initiatives' and realize that none of that makes any sense if your front-line employees 'don't give a damn.' Eric Chester provides a compelling resource in this comprehensive and practical book."

Rhoda Olsen, President, Great Clips, Inc.

"A must-read for any manager looking to grow, succeed, and be one step ahead in their field. It clearly teaches today's managers *how* to build a fun and productive environment in which Gen Whys can truly enjoy their after-school jobs. Follow Eric Chester's advice and watch your business grow through sales, profits, and people!"

Michael Scruggs, Senior Vice President–Global Operations, Little Caesars Pizza

"Front-line workers are making a real difference in many American organizations. Leaders need to understand their significance and motivate them to achieve—that's what *Getting Them to Give a Damn* is all about!"

**Marshall Goldsmith, PhD, coeditor/author of *The Leader of the Future* and
*The Art and Practice of Leadership Coaching***

"In this highly competitive business environment, the absolute silver bullet to sustainable long-term success is in finding top young talent and getting them to consistently deliver kick-ass service. Eric Chester is clearly inside the head of today's front-line worker, and this book will take you there and show you how to connect with them so they will connect with your guests. Humorous, thought-provoking, and 'spot on' with its observations, this book rocks!"

Jim Knight, Director of Training, Hard Rock International

"Corporations have changed, and far more work is done by low-cost labor. And that labor is either overseas or it's young. And the young are playing by different rules today. In this book, Eric Chester tells you the truth. He'll explain to you how vital it is that you get the right people doing the right things. And then he'll show you what they want—no, *demand*—from you in order for you to get what you want. If you want to succeed in these crazy times, you *need* this book."

**Seth Godin, Author of *Purple Cow, Permission Marketing*, and
*All Marketers Are Liars***

"Eric offers an intense review on the art of inspiring and leading younger employees and explains how to turn them into one of your strongest assets. His experiences with youth make this study a valuable tool for any manager with a young workforce."

Nido Qubein, Chairman, Great Harvest Bread Company, and President, High Point University

"As an employer of over 40,000 sixteen- to twenty-four-year-olds, I could definitely relate when reading this book. The days of 'my way or the highway' and 'be available when I need you' management are gone. Your success depends on their success. Every business owner, corporate executive, and manager who relies on young talent to build sales and make money needs to read *Getting Them to Give a Damn!*"

Mark Flores, Executive Vice President and Director of Operations, Chuck E. Cheese

C o n t e n t s

Acknowledgments   vii

Preface   ix

PART ONE
The "Then" versus "Now" Perspective

1. THE PAGODA PRINCIPLE   3
2. WHO'S CALLING THE SHOTS?   8
3. VALUESQUAKE: THE SHIFT IN WORK ETHIC   17
4. THE "GIVE A DAMN" CONTINUUM   26

PART TWO
How to Attract Them

5. THE OPIE IDEAL   37
6. IDENTIFYING OPIES   42
7. RECRUITING OPIES   49

PART THREE
How to Keep Them

 8. RETENTION: HANG ON FOR DEAR LIFE   61
 9. COMPENSATION: SHARE THE LOVE   68
10. RECOGNITION: DOES ANYONE NOTICE?   78
11. MANAGEMENT STYLE: ZAG TO AVOID THE DRAG   88
12. TURNOVER: SLOWING DOWN THE ENDLESS
     TREADMILL   95

PART FOUR
How to Connect with Them

13. ORIENTATION AND TRAINING: BUY IN FROM DAY ONE   109
14. COMMUNICATION: LAYING DOWN THE LAW AND KEEPING IT   117
15. HONESTY: IT'S THE BEST POLICY. WHAT'S YOURS?   128
16. MENTORSHIP: SIMON SAYS, "LEAD THE WAY"   137
17. SERVICE: KEEPING YOUR YOUNGEST EMPLOYEES FROM DRIVING AWAY YOUR OLDEST CUSTOMERS   146

PART FIVE
Who's Getting It Right?

18. STONE COLD CRAZY KIDPLOYEES   159
19. OPPORTUNITY KNOCKS AT SOUTHWESTERN   166
20. U.S. ARMY: BUY IN OF THE HIGHEST ORDER   173
21. A GREAT JOB FLIPPIN' BURGERS?   179
22. AND ONE TO GROW ON   186

Index   199
About the Author   207

The insights and ideas in the pages that follow have come from my experience of working with young people all of my professional life. I am forever grateful for the opportunities I have been given to speak for them but confess that I have learned more from them than they have from me. Since I founded Generation Why, Inc., in 1997, I have worked with some amazing individuals and with some truly great companies and organizations. While there are too many to list, I am indebted to each of them.

Special thanks to my sister and research assistant Christie Chester; my business mentor Mark Sanborn; my editor Barbara McNichol; my colleague TJ Schier; my visibility coach David Avrin; contributors Tawnya Lassiter, Karen LaFonda, and Lee McCroskey; and to the great team at Dearborn Trade Publishing.

A very special thanks to my children for allowing me to learn through their experiences and to tell their stories, and to my awesome wife, Lori, for her continual support and encouragement.

Give a Damn \Giv • ə • dam\ *vb* 1: CARE. 2: To feel a sense of personal obligation. 3: To commit oneself fully to a job, pursuit, or cause. *see also* BUY IN

This book is about successfully employing teenagers and 20-somethings. As of this writing, this group was born between the years of 1980 and 1994, a segment of the American population I refer to as "Generation Why." However, as I have come to believe through my research and writings, inherent dangers lurk when generalizing about a group of individuals born between certain years. While such generalizations make for interesting dialogue and comparisons, this type of demography is far from an exact science.

Research designed to spell out the differences among people in various generations can't be exact. Obviously, there's no way to say that a child born on December 31, 1979, is a typical Generation Xer, while somebody born the next day is a prototype Generation Why. No single day, week, month, year, or even span of years can accurately describe or predict the behavior of individuals born therein.

Rather, researchers base generational studies on shared historical perspectives. While I personally agree with much of what is being written, I recognize that some of the characteristics used to label people don't always hold water.

So instead of referring to a particular generation, *Getting Them to Give a Damn* discusses a comparison between "then" and "now." Things are different "now" than they were "then"—"then" referring to when you and I grew up. Remember back when everyone was talking about jitterbugging? Or was it Sputnik? Ringo? Vietnam? Atari? Rodney King? Believe it or not, I work with managers as young as 25 who approach me after a presentation and lament, "What's up with kids these days? I could never have gotten away with the things they're trying to pull off!"

THEN AND NOW

In this book, *then* means the way things used to be in the workforce when life moved at a relatively slow pace, technology wasn't pervasive, the management-labor dichotomy was well-defined, and workers ascribed to traditional values and standards. *Now* refers to the dynamics of today's workplace. *Getting Them to Give a Damn* discusses the realities of employing today's youth—referred to as "kidployees"—who have come of age in the late '90s and beyond.

Please note, therefore, that broad-based references made about generations are intended to contrast the differences in the workplace between then and now. View any mention of the generations, particularly Generation Why, as a shorthand term that encompasses the current members of today's entry-level workforce in general. We could call these people front-liners, but some don't necessarily work on the front line. Indeed, they might have already *passed* the front line in their jobs. Or they might be working on the back lines, having no interface with the customer but still making a vital contribution to their team, department, or company. The back line represents busboys, maids, cooks, laborers, stock clerks, techies, assembly line workers, and so on—people who do their jobs outside of the customer's view. Hence, though the subtitle of this book refers to front-liners who interact with the customer daily, the term *kidployee* includes those who are relatively new to the working world.

I also recognize that, in their day-to-day grind, today's managers and supervisors don't give a flip about specific birth years; they've got sales targets to reach, quotas to fill, reports to complete, and bosses to please. To complicate things, they're overwhelmed with the arduous task of trying to get on the same page with entry-level workers who don't respond to the same strategies and tactics that they did when entering the work force. That's precisely why I wrote this book.

WHY "KIDPLOYEES?"

Getting Them to Give a Damn is about all members of our young, emerging workforce, not simply the 16-year-old who takes your order at the drive-thru. After all, aren't 22-year-old management trainees considered "kids" by their bosses? So I'm not calling these employees *teenagers,* because this book also relates to those in their early 20s. In addition, I can't accurately refer to them as first-jobbers, because legions of employees aged 17 to 19 have already worked in a dozen or more jobs.

The word that managers commonly use when discussing their young workforce is *kids.* When we go to the supermarket, for example, we refer to the young people who bag our groceries as kids. We also talk about the kids making millions playing basketball in the NBA, the kids we rely on to repair our computers, and the kids on an entirely different front line defending our country. The kids in each of these situations can be as young as 16 and as old as 24, plus they are on somebody's payroll, which technically makes them employees. So I playfully use the word *kidployees*—those legally old enough to have a job but too young to know that the words *rap* and *music* don't belong in the same sentence.

To further define 16-year-old to 24-year-old kidployees, they are those who could well be having a first employment experience, either part-time or full-time. A kidployee could currently be in high school, have graduated from high school, have recently come out of a technical or trade school, or be going to college. Yes, a kidployee could even be a college graduate seeking their first "real" job.

You might assume that most kidployees are employed by the retail industry, particularly in fast food, grocery, and restaurant services. Yet millions work in offices, in warehouses, in call centers, as sales professionals, in customer service, as van or truck drivers, in health care, for non-for-profit organizations, and in government. They could even be married with kids of their own.

KIDPLOYEES EVERYWHERE

It's difficult to find any business or service that doesn't have a front-line staff someplace in their operations. In certain professions such as advanced medicine, rocket telemetry, and biochemistry, employees tend to be more mature; they have graduate degrees and perhaps several years of experience. Kidployees are not found within these ranks, yet these fields are still directly or indirectly affected by kidployees.

In health care, for example, a sizable number of kidployees enter the field as nurses, orderlies, maintenance staff, janitorial staff, or receptionists. They might be lab assistants or research assistants; they might work in billing, in the cafeteria, or in shipping and receiving.

Kidployees are commonly found in the tech sector. They've grown up immersed in megabits and microchips, and the tech industry seeks innovative young employees to fuel their projects. Tech managers often live on the edge and have no qualms about reaching down to the youngest ages of technical talent. In many instances, the younger the better, because kidployees are likely to generate the coolest ideas and freshest approaches.

The same phenomenon is at play in the semiconductor, manufacturing, and pharmaceutical industries. Managers search for new, fresh blood and all the technosavvy that arrives with it. In making such hires, however, they'll inherit the kidployee work ethic, which, I assure you, differs vastly from what many managers wish it to be.

WHY THIS INFORMATION IS CRUCIAL

In many respects, the manager or supervisor seeking information about hiring and successfully retaining today's youth doesn't have many resources to tap. Those working in large organizations might turn to case histories or FAQs that have been placed on their own company's intranet—to their great advantage. But most managers don't have such resources at their fingertips. Perhaps they've clipped articles from newspapers and magazines, found useful Web sites, and talked to other managers. But in general, they find it difficult to round up information on how to encourage young workers to give a damn about their jobs. These managers simply haven't known where to turn—until now. *Getting Them to Give a Damn* serves as an all-purpose FAQ and answer guide, delivering valuable insights and ideas that work.

Part One

THE "THEN" VERSUS "NOW" PERSPECTIVE

You Can't Get Them to Give a Damn
If You Don't Know Why They Don't

1

THE PAGODA PRINCIPLE

The young boy's first ever job was washing dishes at a mom-and-pop Chinese restaurant a few blocks from his home. At age 15, he was lucky that the owner gave him a shot.

He worked Monday through Friday from 5:00 PM to 9:00 PM and got his weekly take-home pay in 20 one-dollar bills. He knew his dollar-an-hour salary wasn't much, even by early 1970s standards, but it wasn't bad considering he was paid under the table. Besides, he was happy just to have a job. Working at the restaurant sure as heck wasn't a career position, but he was determined to do a good job and make his dad proud of him. While most kids would have spent their earnings on games or candy, he planned on saving every cent from his first four weeks—a total of $80—to buy an airplane ticket and visit his best friend, who'd moved 1,000 miles away at the end of eighth grade.

Monday through Thursday, business was slow and he had only a few dishes to wash. This should have translated into easy money for the kid, but the restaurant's owner/operator, Mr. Wong, was determined to give him a crash course on work ethic. Wong continually stood over the boy and browbeat him, working him at a feverish pitch as if the place were on fire. The kid barely had time to catch his breath as the owner barked commands in broken English. "Sweep storeroom—no crumbs for tiniest of mice!" "Fill all ketchup bottles, and salt and pepper shakers!" "Scrape the gum from underneath all tables. I want them as clean as top side!"

And despite having a brand new electric dishwasher, Mr. Wong refused to let the kid use it, making him wash every dish by hand.

Specifically, Mr. Wong never called the boy by his first name or asked him about school, his family, his girlfriend, or his free-time activities. He said little about himself or his own life and made it clear that any communication unrelated to the job was completely unnecessary. Obviously, Wong believed that as long as he paid the wages, he made the rules.

> The workload might have been bearable, if the owner had made any kind of personal connection with the kid, but he treated him as his personal whipping boy.

If the kid completed a task short of perfection, Wong jumped all over him. "Whatsa matter with you? You cannot do no mediocre job, here!" he chided. And for all the chores that the 15-year-old handled, Wong never once offered a kind word or encouraging statement.

Every Friday, the pace of business increased dramatically as the restaurant filled to capacity. Those were the nights the kid was hit with stacks of dishes from the instant he came in to the second before he walked out the door. All that time, he received no break or snack, not even an occasional fortune cookie.

Within his first four weeks, the boy became totally frustrated with his job, his boss, and the whole concept of a part-time job. On his way home one Thursday evening, already dreading the Friday night ordeal, he realized he was only one night's work away from being able to buy the $80 plane ticket. So he came up with a scheme to punctuate his resignation.

After school on Friday, using supplies from his father's art studio, he created a professional-looking sign that read:

CLOSED BY ORDER OF HEALTH DEPARTMENT

At 4:55 PM, he showed up for work at the restaurant, put on his apron, and started to work. In the meantime, he'd arranged to have his buddy walk by the restaurant at 5:15 PM and tape the *Closed* sign to the front door.

The sign proved to be convincing because that Friday night, the place was empty. Mr. Wong became anxious, more so with each passing hour. He got so caught up trying to figure out why he had no customers that he completely ignored his hired help. But even if he had wanted to take out his tension by browbeating his young employee, there was little left to do. The storeroom had been swept, the ketchup bottles and salt and pepper shakers had been filled, and the gum had already been scraped from underneath the tables. After 19 consecutive evenings of feeling like a prisoner in a gulag, the kid finally got his first break, and his revenge tasted as sweet as the fortune cookies he was sneaking out of the storage room bins.

Around 8:30 that evening, Mr. Wong finally discovered the sign on his door and realized he had been the victim of a cruel prank. Furious and highly suspicious, he began interrogating his employee. Anticipating this, the boy shrugged his shoulders and denied any involvement, but his face was ridden with guilt. Wong knew who was directly responsible. He angrily reached deep into his pocket, pulled out 20 one-dollar bills from a money clip, and slapped them into the boy's hand. Then he shook his finger at the kid and scolded, "Don't you come back to Pagoda again!"

Angry and upset? No way! The boy skipped home with a bulging pocket and a huge smile on his face. At that moment, he was probably the happiest outsourced, downsized, laid off, totally fired employee in the history of the free world.

As for Mr. Wong, he lost a lot of business that Friday night. Every business owner reading this must feel some compassion for his plight. After all, no matter how bad the situation becomes, an employee can always quit. But to go to the extreme of putting your employer out of business for a whole evening—that's treason!

TRUE CONFESSION

I'll spare you the mystery. I am the 15-year-old boy in this story, and I'm not proud of what I did to Mr. Wong back in 1972. But I share this with you for good reason.

Although my father and I were close, this stunt that involved his art supplies when I was a 15-year-old first jobber was the one story I could never tell him before he passed away in 2003. Dad put up with my adolescent pranks and got me out of more jams than I care to remember, but I know he'd never let me get away with this one. Even now, as I come clean about what I did to Mr. Wong at the Pagoda Restaurant, I'm sure Dad is rolling over in his grave.

My dad, W. Grant Chester—born in 1921 and raised during the Great Depression—valued work above all else. As a teen, he stood in long bread lines and begged for work. As a result, he never ever took a paycheck for granted. Dad believed that the employer rightfully maintained supreme authority over the employee. It didn't matter if you disliked your boss; you did as you were told to the best of your ability. Dad taught my four sisters and me always to show respect and to keep our mouths shut, our eyes open, and our noses to the grindstone. He insisted that we give our bosses all we had and take pride in doing our jobs well, no matter what. He said we'd always have opportunities to advance. If we worked hard, kept our heads down, and bided our time, good things would happen.

THAT WAS THEN, THIS IS NOW

My own story begs this question: if a kid raised by a father who so deeply ingrained "giving a damn" into his young psyche could look past these lessons and hang a *Closed* sign on his employer's front door, to what lengths would today's disgruntled young employees go to make a statement against their employers?

Scary thought, huh?

Add to the equation the fact that many parents today spend much less face time with their children than in days gone by. Even when they do, the lessons they teach rarely touch on valuing jobs and giving employers their all. Worse, many kids are taught *not* to give a damn. Rather, they learn to put their own needs above those of their employers. Kids in today's world often hear their parents and teachers complain about their own jobs and how they want a bigger, better deal somewhere else.

Boomers and Gen Xers like us are known to work extremely hard to give their kids material things and promote self-actualization. As a group, we love our children and care deeply about their futures. Conveying a work ethic to them, however, is too often lacking from our family discussions.

The work ethic is rarely enforced in our schools, either. Today, citizens demand academic accountability from their community schools. Independent agencies evaluate schools periodically and publish comparative scores in the local newspaper. We want to find out how schools in our own neighborhood stack up against those across the county line. This mandates that educators forgo the relationship building of days gone by, instead using every available minute to "teach to the test" so that their students can fill in the correct bubble on rigorous standardized achievement tests. Forget preparing a kid for the world of work; that's not on the exam.

This means that, as an employer of 16- to 24-year-olds, you commonly staff your front lines with kids who are streetwise, booksmart, and technosavvy, but who don't really give a damn about jobs that don't appear—at least to them at the time—directly related to their ultimate dream career position. It's a position, incidentally, that they've been promised "if they simply think big and believe in themselves," or they even think they can win it on a reality television show.

Make no mistake: getting your young employees to give a damn about you, your business, your customers, and their jobs isn't easy. They're simply not wired that way.

But you needn't check to see if there's a sign on your front door just yet.

2

WHO'S CALLING
THE SHOTS?

Up until the economic boom of the early '90s, who was in the driver's seat of the employment equation in America? Companies. They had the jobs. Bosses in these companies decided who got hired and who didn't. If you wanted to land a job, you knew you had better clean up, buck up, suck up, and shut up. If you were a kid who got on at the local market, you'd brag about it to your friends and they'd ask, "Hey, can you put in a good word for me and get me on, too?"

Today's new service economy has changed all that. While our parents were primarily do-it-yourselfers, you and I as Baby Boomers and Gen Xers hire work out. We want our houses painted, our windows washed, and our lawns mowed by someone else. We'd like to have our cars washed and our pizza brought to our front doors. Plus, we find it easy to drop off our young ones at day care when we need free time.

We're not about to do anything ourselves that we can get somebody else to do for less money than we consider our own "going rate." Our parents were of a different persuasion. Need further proof? I bet your dad changed the oil and tuned up your family's car(s), and your mom baked your birthday cakes from scratch. Do you?

With the service sector booming and no end in sight, where have companies turned to find labor for those jobs? You guessed it, teenagers.

This means that, unlike you and I, our kids believe their services are in high demand and that jobs are a dime a dozen. To them, the landscape has always been dotted with *Help Wanted* signs of every variety. They believe that if anyone is calling the shots in the employment equation, it's them, not the bosses. Can you blame them?

The way they see it, if you want them to work for you, you'd better be nice, offer better wages than the guy down the street, be flexible and considerate of their "me time," and have a long list of "perks" and "bennies" to dangle in front of them. Above all, you'd better show them respect and avoid saying anything that might offend them.

THE "US/THEM; THEN/NOW" QUADRANT

Unless you're a student reading this book as an assignment or a young person trying to understand the adults in your life, I assume you are one of "us" and come from the world of "then." This book is about "them"—today's 16- to 24-year-olds who only comprehend the world of "now." They have no reference for how it was back then for us. How could they?

For practical purposes, the "Us versus Them; Then versus Now" terminology is shorthand that helps us compare today's workplace with yesterday's.

Us	Them
Then	Now

Us Back Then

Regardless whether you fall into the category of a Traditionalist, Baby Boomer, or Generation Xer, you're from one of these three current generations who were born before 1980. Odds are, you were raised with—or at least had knowledge of—the work ethic referred to here, even if you never called it that.

The work ethic you grew up with meant that you valued work and valued your job. You put your best into your job; you dressed and played the part with sincerity. When your boss said "jump," you asked "how high?" Because it was routinely grilled into you that "customer is king," you treated customers like royalty—and felt entitled to the same treatment when you stood on the opposite side of the counter.

> We have no idea that the people working for us could actually be working against us. When we look closely at our enemies, sometimes we see people on our own team, the same people we hired.

This work ethic prevailed whether you aspired to be a business owner or a truck driver, a police officer or a ballerina, a knee surgeon or a tree surgeon. When you walked through your company's front door and put on that uniform, you transcended your own personality and assumed the role for which you were hired. You rolled up your shirtsleeves and got busy.

You were raised in an era when jobs defined what people did, how they felt, and who they were. You heard people introduce themselves by their titles, saying, "I'm an accountant," or, "I'm a seamstress," or, "I'm a plumber," and so on. You knew that someday your job would also define you, so a solid work ethic became entrenched in your psyche in hopes of becoming a grown-up—the sooner the better.

Them Right Now

Today, employers everywhere complain that their emerging frontliners have no concept of the work ethic and little regard for their jobs. Further, young workers get ticked off at the slightest provocation. They prioritize their jobs below their social activities and resist adhering to company dress code standards. They don't like to be reprimanded, rarely take criticism well, and expect raises regardless of how well the company is doing. And God forbid what could happen if a kidployee decides to "even up the score" after a perceived transgression.

NO SOUP FOR YOU

Today's kidployees are simply not taught to give a damn. Or, worse, they're specifically taught *not* to give a damn. The distinction isn't subtle. They're not instructed to show they should care, buy in, and give a damn. What's more, all too often they are taught clearly: don't care, don't buy in, don't give a damn at all.

What's the evidence? Listen for their sea of catchphrases such as:

- "Stick it to the man."
- "Make sure it works for you."

- "What's in it for me?"
- "You deserve the very best."
- "Take all you can get."
- "Look out for number one."
- "Don't take nothin' from nobody!"
- "You ain't nobody's bitch."

Some kidployees play out the classic line, "No soup for you," from a *Seinfeld* episode in which a local food merchant known as the "soup Nazi" decides who among his customers will have their soup order filled and who will be turned away. When they use the phrase *no soup for you,* front-line service providers are deciding which patron gets what and when.

Even if the phrase *no soup for you* is never uttered, its sentiment flourishes, because the kidployee who ultimately determines which customer receives adequate service and which one gets stonewalled. No matter how good your "soup" is, if you leave an unsupervised 16-year-old with an attitude in charge of cooking it, doling it out, and collecting money for it, you're begging for trouble.

"Sticking it to the man" seems to be the message that kidployees have picked up, often through no fault of their own. Their parents might have complained about a work situation, or their teachers and coaches might convey that they have their eyes open for better deals somewhere else. Pop music and media messages suggest that, "To win in life, you've got to get more than you put in." No wonder teens often brag to their friends about finding a "piece-o-cake" job that doesn't require much effort to get a paycheck.

Vast numbers of kidployees have been provided with all of the comfort and material needs they could possibly want. Their Baby-Boomer or Gen-X parents work hard to ensure that their kids don't lack anything that they can provide.

Clearly, these parents don't instill the work ethic in their kids. Instead, they focus on the children's self-esteem and ability to feel good while coping in a noisy, crowded, overcommunicated world. The irony of teaching self-esteem instead of a work ethic is that true self-esteem comes from pride of accomplishment, which is only assured after hard work and sacrifice.

> To the kidployees with no work ethic, a job is merely a means to an end. And they regard all jobs as temporary.

AND YOU'RE SPECIAL, TOO!

About 130 years ago, a kidployee's biggest self-esteem-building moments involved things like riding on top of a full corn wagon or watching the water flow from a newly assembled well. Thirty years ago, such moments came from finishing yard work or helping dad clean the garage. Today, a kid's self-esteem is rooted in the "bling" they can flash, the dance moves they can bust, and the high score they can get on a video game. And by the time they turn ten, mom and dad have told them, "You're special," so many times, they believe at the core level that they're entitled to extraordinary treatment and rewards.

From a purely economic standpoint, whether kids have jobs or not, they'll still acquire the stuff they want and need because their parents, one way or another, see to it. My friends reside in a highly affluent area of Denver. Their biggest social challenge is finding a babysitter, because the 13- and 14-year-olds in their neighborhood simply don't need the money they'd earn from babysitting. Whether it's $5 an hour at stake or even twice that much, young teens think, "I don't need the money that badly, and I sure don't want to give up my Friday night."

WHEN KIDS HAVE EVERYTHING, WHY GET A JOB?

If there are no real needs, no incentives, and certainly no one pushing them, why would a dependent teen ever want a job? Why take a ten-dollar-an-hour babysitting post? After all, mom and dad have the means to give the kid everything: a laptop, a cell phone, an mp3 player, a motorized scooter, a car, and plenty of running-around cash. Today, even 12-year-olds are handed credit cards in their own names with the assurance that mom and dad will pay the tab.

Statistics prove that this phenomenon isn't limited to families living in affluent areas. Look around. Even in middle-class and lower-class neighborhoods, kids sport $100 athletic jerseys, iPods, cell phones, and all kinds of other desirable (and expensive) stuff. If you were to add up the price of all the items found in a kid's bedroom today, it would dwarf what a kid of 20, 30, or 40 years ago owned by a factor of 25 times or more. Realistically, kids couldn't earn a sum of money equal to all these goods anyway—the snowboard, the CDs, the X-Box, the Air Jordans, the makeup kits, or the low-cut designer jeans. And they know it.

Guilt and Money

Kay Hymowitz, author of *Liberation's Children,* notes that parents today lavish their children with Tommy Hilfiger clothing, Game Boys, and Disneyland vacations but don't know how to provide them with "the ordinary truths that give meaning to life." Without a coherent moral and intellectual order to pass on to the young, Hymowitz says, "Parents, teachers, school principals, the media, and the childrearing experts know only how to celebrate the individual child—while many young people flounder in a spiritual and imaginative void."

Many parents heap material goods on their children because they suffer from guilt-earned wealth. Those who spend an inordinate amount of time at work take the fruit of their labor—proceeds from their jobs—and spend extra money on their kids. They think these goods can atone for lack of time together hanging out, taking walks, shooting hoops, and playing games.

When Face Time Is Lacking

Even though their closets are overflowing, many of today's youth have spirits that are empty, because what they truly need and want can't be bought, sold, or traded on eBay. When having the face time they crave with mom and/or dad isn't available, they collect more stuff hoping to fill the void they feel.

Contrast this predicament with what happened back then. You and I grew up in an era when the typical kid spent considerably more time with one or both parents than kids do today. Dinnertime was family time; bedtime was story time. When the family television was on, our parents watched it with us. When the phone rang, it was regarded as an interruption in our family conversation. You and I had our parents' attention to be sure, although we didn't own anywhere near the same amount of stuff as our children own.

I vividly remember the Christmas when I was hoping my buddy would get a train set. Because I had four sisters and parents who earned a modest income, it went beyond my comprehension to think I'd ever receive one, so playing with a train set at a friend's house was good enough for me. That was then. Now, getting a train set (or whatever the contemporary equivalent might be) is a sure thing. Whether the parents put it on a credit card or take out a second mortgage on the house, it's a virtual certainty that the kid won't go without their heart's desire.

YOU GOT A JOB . . . SO WHAT?

When I was a teenager and one of my friends landed a job, everyone regarded their accomplishment as a big deal. My friend would run home and announce, "Mom! Dad! I got hired at the grocery store!" and receive congratulatory hugs from all around and phone calls from the grandparents. Most likely, a celebration dinner followed. Then, when friends heard the news, they'd scurry down to the same store and put in their applications.

Now, kids are expected to work, and many feel entitled to have a job automatically. The conversation would go like this:

"Yo ma, I won't be home until late tomorrow. I took a job at the supermarket."

"Oh yeah, how much you gettin'?"

The demand for workers is so high that, as soon as new employees start their jobs, their managers or human resources directors ask about friends who might also be looking for work.

It Doesn't A.D.D. Up

Then, young employees felt appreciative, upbeat, and enthusiastic at work. Today, managers lament that their front-liners are moody, if not outright despondent.

Theoretically, the quality of life for these kids should be the highest it's ever been for any generation in our history. By any economic analysis, they have more—much more—than any previous group. Sadly, they feel more anxious and stressed than kids of any other age. The pressures of handling school, friends, and social activities have been thrust upon them with little parental involvement. Many feel overwhelmed. Further, they're continually pounded with messages promising instant gratification from purveyors of alcohol, tobacco, gambling, sex, and pharmaceuticals.

Alarmingly, statistics from the pharmaceutical industry show that more kids than ever take prescription medication, most often antidepressants. Many take Ritalin to counter hyperactivity or attention deficit disorder (A.D.D.), while Prozac and Zoloft are commonly prescribed for moodiness. Overmedicated kids, either too depressed or too hyper to cope with everyday realities, comprise a huge segment of today's young labor pool.

You can see how all of this might wreak havoc with the emerging workforce's work ethic and the idea of authority, service, and loyalty. For them, a job is simply a "thing" kids have to do to acquire "stuff" (if they can't get what they want any other way). Company loyalty has become an oxymoron, because they see a need to build a résumé and constantly move on. They think, "No one has the right to ask me to do anything that's beneath me. I'm special, and if I'm not treated accordingly, I'll go someplace where people will celebrate my uniqueness and reward me." Those who exude this attitude will return kindness when it's given to them, but if they perceive that someone disrespects them, they'll get in that person's face immediately.

As Dorothy muttered to her dog Toto in the classic film *The Wizard of Oz,* "We're not in Kansas anymore!" However, understanding the challenges you face with your front-line employees is, by itself, not enough. For you to relate to them, you also need to know *why* the challenges exist. The pool of young talent is deep; its skills and abilities fall nothing short of amazing. But to harvest those talents and get kids producing for you, it's essential that you understand how the Us/Then; Them/Now (UTTN) Quadrant has affected the modern-day kidployee work ethic.

THE FEW, THE PROUD, THE FOREIGN BORN

A notable exception to this phenomenon of the declining work ethic among front-line employees is that of immigrants, particularly those from the Pacific Rim and the Middle East. When you pull up to a convenience store or call tech support for a computer problem, you're likely to encounter a Korean, East Indian, or Pakistani behind the counter or over the phone. This young man or woman generally comes across as being grateful for the job and eager to please both the boss and the customer.

Their storylines don't follow the script of second-, third-, or fourth-generation immigrants. Their parents likely work as long and as hard (if not longer and harder) than the American-born grandparents of home-grown kidployees. The senior members of the family convey the traditional values of work: holding a job, being responsible to an employer, showing up on time, and serving the customer well. In fact, the work experience itself might be as valuable to these immigrants as the income, if not more so. Plus their parents and grandparents would be mortified if they discovered that their sons or daughters got fired from a position. Certainly, these young employees would do anything to avoid shaming their families.

How Changes in Society's Values Have Impacted the Work Ethic in America

Us	Them
Parents were dedicated to the company.	Parents complain about work.
Parents/Schools taught work ethic.	Parents/Schools don't teach the work ethic.
Work hard . . . feel proud . . . get ahead!	Work hard . . . feel tired . . . miss out!
Adults were defined by their vocation.	Adults are defined by wealth and leisure time.
The customer was king.	Customers are equal, not elevated.
Dress for success.	Personal image is everything.
Buy in to the company credo.	Don't sell out to anyone at any time.
Get on with a good company that takes care of you.	Every company will eventually outsource you or automate your job.
You climbed the corporate ladder and retired with a pension.	You build your résumé with vast experience from many jobs and retire with an IRA.

Then	Now
Teens had to work to buy a car and cool stuff.	Parents give teens a car and other cool stuff.
Jobs for teens were hard to find.	Jobs for teens are in endless supply.
The boss was the boss.	The boss is your peer, if not your buddy.
Employers were to be respected above all.	Employees are to be respected above all.
School first, then job, then friends/activities.	Friends/activities first, then school, then job.
Unethical employees were fired, vilified.	Unethical employees can become CEO.
A kid is a kid is a kid. "You're no different than anyone else. If you want to achieve great things, you have to work harder than the next guy."	Every kid is a gift from God. "You're special. You're destined to do great things and have it all someday, because no one else in the world is exactly like you."

3

VALUESQUAKE: THE SHIFT IN WORK ETHIC

Us versus Them. Now versus Then. I can just imagine what you're thinking: "Hey! I've got a business to run! When I entered the workforce as a teen, I wasn't exactly like my parents, either. I may not have been an Opie, but I knew how to get ahead. I had to clean up, listen up, and suck up. It was sink or swim. And if I wanted to keep my job and keep my parents off my back, I had to learn to do what I was told, work hard, and not miss a day, or I'd be out on my ear. Now that I'm a manager, you're telling me to throw out my rulebook and reinvent my entire business, just to cater to a bunch of whiney, spoiled-rotten prima donnas? Forget it!"

Slow down, Speed Racer. No one's suggesting that you throw out anything. All we have to agree on at this point are the following three assertions:

1. The employment picture for 16- to 24-year-olds has changed since you were in this age range.
2. The 16- to 24-year-olds you encounter in the workplace today have a different set of attitudes, values, and beliefs than young people of days gone by.
3. Today's kidployees can't be recruited, trained, managed, and motivated the same way you were as a kidployee.

In theory, statement three is easy to agree with but very hard to act on. It could make you feel even more conflicted. To take a different course of action would mean accepting that a better one exists—or worse, that you're doing something wrong in your present course. Because you're used to doing things a certain way, to change goes against the grain. Nobody likes change—except for a wet baby.

When I accepted my first teaching assignment back in 1979, the principal began the school year by having the teachers arrive a day before the students. After coffee and donuts, we went to the band room to listen to a motivational speaker. This first exposure to a professional speaker impressed me. His clever one-liners and stories were designed to "rally the troops" and get our hearts ready for the challenge of a new year. Looking back, I forget most of what he said, but I do remember one powerful axiom he left with us that day. He said:

"If you do what you've always done, you will get what you've always gotten."

That sounded so cool and seemed so logical that I wrote it down on my lesson plan book and internalized it. It became a basic tenant in the way I led my life and approached my daily activities. Twenty-five years later, I still believe it's true . . . for plumbers and tree surgeons, that is.

You see, over time, pipes and trees haven't changed much—but people have. Just as an earthquake occurs due to a shift in the ground beneath us, there a "valuesquake" has happened because of a major shift in societal values and norm's beneath us. There is no arguing that those shifts are clearly reflected in the attitudes and beliefs of our children. So the axiom I wrote on my lesson plan book in 1979 has been proven false. In fact, today I believe the following axiom is much more accurate:

If you do what you've always done, you are out of business.

You simply can't successfully manage today's kidployees using yesterday's management methodologies. The employment picture has changed, and so have they. The emerging workforce isn't motivated by the same things; they cannot be communicated with, compensated, motivated, and disciplined with old-school techniques.

Platinum Rule

Business strategist and bestselling author Dr. Tony Alessandra has said that the Golden Rule—"Do unto others as you would have them do unto you"—has been trumped by the Platinum Rule—"Do unto others as *they* would have you do unto *them*." The Golden Rule implies that other people would like to be treated the way that you would like to be treated. The Platinum Rule encourages us to treat others the way *they* want to be treated.

Leading managers realize that, to get the most out of their work-force, they must first determine who *the workers* are and what they want done unto *them*. For kidployees, it's important to understand what their attitudes and beliefs really are. How are they wired?

This chapter examines four primary differences between you and your front-line workforce. You know these differences exist, but perhaps you've never understood why. Nothing happens overnight, yet in the past decade, a monumental shift—or valuesquake—has occurred, dramatically impacting the mindset of the new workforce. Let's dissect four of these shifts to see how they have quaked the attitudes and beliefs that kidployees bring to the job, forming a base for addressing strategies and tactics in future chapters. They are:

1. A shift toward digital thinking
2. A shift in the importance of self-expression
3. A shift in the way the game is played
4. A shift from a traditional work ethic

A SHIFT TOWARD DIGITAL THINKING

A profound difference between you and the new breed of kidployee is the way they think and process information. While your mind operates more like a VCR, theirs functions more like a DVD player. Although both devices process complex sights and sounds, one accesses information in a sequential order, while the other can access and process it sequentially, in reverse, or in random order with no loss of time.

You're probably reading this book much like you do the morning paper—from the front to the back. I bet you eat your salad before your steak and your steak before dessert. Similarly, when you accepted your first job with your organization, you expected to begin low and work your way up through the ranks. With any new recreational pursuit, you fully expected to start out as a beginner, pay your dues as an intermediate, and consistently practice and move to the next level.

As linear, or analog, thinkers and doers, you and I tend to move sequentially from left to right, from top to bottom, from front to back. We've been taught to learn, earn, save, then spend. Our parents ingrained into our psyches the need to work before we could play. You and I believe in a natural order of things, the law of the farm: cultivate, plant, fertilize, then harvest.

Your front-liners don't see life that way. For them, life is an all-you-can-eat buffet offering unlimited choice, few rules, and a pay-as-you-go system. They see absolutely no reason to stick with our "analog" logic in this "digital" world—not when they believe in their ability to leapfrog over the painstaking cultivate, plant, and fertilize steps and go directly to the harvest.

Wired for Choices

How could any manager expect employees who were value-programmed over the past 20 years to be remotely the same as we were? How could we expect them to think sequentially when they're wired for a pull-down menu of choices and immediate results? If they don't think like us, they aren't automatically in sync with our logic, rules, practices, and procedures.

As an analog thinker (us), you understand the actual flow of life—everything you do at this moment yields a future result. You and I grew up in a time that reinforced the dynamic of choice and consequence, cause and effect. Do your homework and get a good grade. Commit a crime and go to jail. Work hard and get ahead. Our decisions were, and still are, made with future considerations in mind.

However, to a digital thinker (them), the principle of choice followed by consequence has lost its power. They know that the good guy often gets the short end of the stick; they've seen the bad guy get away with it too many times. Even though they've been cautioned to consider the logical outcome of their actions, they look for ways to avoid the consequences of their behavior—a loophole. For them, hard work and sacrifice don't always return a high yield. Doing a bad deed doesn't always lead to disciplinary action. Any mistake is wiped over by simply pressing control-alt-delete.

This basic difference in how they are wired gives you reason to completely rethink your managerial philosophies. What choice do you have?

Failing to understand the way a digital mind functions and adjust for it will lead to frustration and an automatic disconnect.

A SHIFT IN THE IMPORTANCE OF SELF-EXPRESSION

Teenage rebellion is nothing new. You and I rebelled against our parents; our parents rebelled against theirs. Even Cain and Abel rebelled against Adam and Eve. The expression *Don't trust anyone over 30* was coined in the 1960s. You can expect a certain degree of rebellion from the 16- to 24-year-olds you employ, right?

But it's the degree of their outspokenness, their refusal to play by the rules, their utter disrespect for authority that prompts you to shake your head and think, "I could never have gotten away with that when I was their age!"

Evidence Abounds

When was the last time a kid stood up to give you a seat on the bus or addressed you as Mr. or Ms. instead of by your first name or, even worse, "Hey you!" How often do you catch a kid doing something they shouldn't be doing but feel deathly afraid of confronting the behavior?

Your front-line digital thinkers have seen how being outrageous leads to fame and fortune. They've also watched nice guys get steamrolled. Further, they've been told that if they want something or if they have an opinion, they'd better speak up and not hold anything back. The new breed of television talk shows has shown them that those who might feel slandered, cheated, or disrespected have the right to confront the perpetrators and give them a piece of their mind. Being rude, crude, obnoxious, and insulting in modern-day America draws laughter, attention, applause, and sometimes even a fat endorsement contract.

Sadly, the virtues of courtesy, tact, and diplomacy are on the endangered species list. Today's 16- to 24-year-olds have their own thoughts, ideas, and opinions—and you are going to hear them, like it or not. They won't stand by passively if they feel they're being disrespected in any way. If a coworker, supervisor, or customer does something to ruffle their feathers, you can bet the conflict goes public. The feedback, which is often personal and negative, can come out at the worst times and in the worst places.

Treated Like Equals

I often hear businesspeople complain that their young talent has no regard for experience and that they arrive on Day One wanting to be treated on a par with senior management. Perhaps because their interests and desires have always been catered to by advertisers, media conglomerates, and even parents, they're used to being sought after. Focus groups seek their opinions, and marketers especially listen very, very carefully to what they think is cool or lame.

And don't think for a moment that your kidployees don't value respect themselves. On the contrary, they know all too well what respect is and, more importantly, the power it holds. They live by the creed: "They who have the respect have the power." To them, respect is a prize that must be won.

Kidployees who crave respect will go to great lengths to get it, but when it comes to giving respect, you might find them stingy. They won't automatically respect you simply because of your age, position, or title. They don't want to yield their power or put you in a position of control over them. In a strange reversal of the traditional dynamic between youth and age, they believe that they're owed respect automatically—but that you have to prove that you're worthy of their consideration. In most situations, respect is bartered. "You respect me first," they seem to be saying, "then maybe I'll respect you."

Obviously, this issue affects your workplace. Perhaps you feel like you've hired a kid who acted very respectfully during the interview and early stages of training, but is actually a Mr. Hyde under the façade, ready to jump out the first time they feel embarrassed, disrespected, or unfairly disciplined.

Dress Code Conflicts

Image is, by far, the largest part of the self-expression equation. Rarely do I speak to a group of managers without the subject of dress code quickly entering the discussion. The prevailing sentiment is this: "We can deal with the hair and the clothes, but how are we supposed to put up with the piercings and the tattoos?" It quite often seems like a stare-down contest requiring one of the two sides to lose big by sacrificing their own appearance for the sake of the other.

What they say, who they respect, and how they dress certainly influences the way you communicate with them and how they interact with your customers. When you have a kidployee who values self-expression over self-control, you could have more than you can handle, regardless of their skill set.

THE SHIFT IN THE WAY THE GAME IS PLAYED

In the summer of 2004, *Spiderman 2* broke all box office records when its opening day took in $116 million in ticket sales. Compare that to *Halo 2*, the video game that came out four months later, which took in $125 million in sales in the first 24 hours. You can see how big video games have become in America.

When I played video games in college, I first conquered *Pong*, then *Space Invaders,* and then I was on to eat dots in the phenomenon of *Pac Man*. It's easy to see how addictive these electronic games can become. Doing well at the video games of my era took fast reflexes, a quick trigger thumb, and a lot of quarters. Today's games are most typically played on in-home game systems. Although they also require fast reflexes, they also require strategy and sophisticated problem-solving skills to win.

Until my son Zac called from college, ecstatic that he had waited in line four hours to be one of the first to buy *Halo 2*, I had never even heard of it. "What makes this game so special?" I wondered. I discovered that it's not just the player against the game, but rather that up to 16 players, located anywhere in the world, can connect online to play the same game simultaneously. This complex war game involves an endless variety of scenarios and possibilities.

Life on the Other Side

As Kevin Maney observed in a *USA Today* article, "The tables have turned, and the axis is videogames. We Boomers have become like those Woodstock town folk we once laughed at. We're on the tragically un-hip side of a generation gap, and the gamers are on the other side." The kidployees in your workforce are the gamers Maney refers to. When it comes to how we each face challenges and solve problems, these kidployees certainly live on the "other side."

Today's video games turn players into stars and feed their egos by heaping praise and rewards on them when they excel. The hero in these games isn't always the honorable character but rather the one who shows the most machismo and bravado. Therefore, players advance only when they act daringly and assume great risk. Strategy and forethought are required to reach the highest levels.

This is the mindset your young workers carry to the front lines. Remember, they won't remain engaged if the job is mundane and boring; you can't get them to invest themselves if they're not challenged to think, react, and affect the outcome of the game. If they can't emerge as stars in your organization, you might as well say, "Tilt—game over."

THE SHIFT AWAY FROM THE TRADITIONAL WORK ETHIC

I first heard my mom use the term *workaholic* to explain why my dad couldn't come watch my football game. He had a tenth-grade education and was the breadwinner for a family of seven, so he was tirelessly trying to make a buck and get ahead. I never saw him take it easy. My father did not have an off switch. By contrast, I wonder if my 20-year-old son even has an on switch.

While I was taught to work by a dad who made sure I'd always pull my weight and learn to survive, I became a dad who wanted his kids to enjoy their childhoods. I took them to places I only dreamed of going when I was a kid and gave them things I wished I had had. Although I never intended to spoil them, they certainly got a lot in exchange for a little.

Not Defined by Work

My hunch (supported by research) tells me that a lot of Baby Boomer/ Generation X parents raised their children like I did. Today, a ton of kid-ployees like Zac and Whitney (my 19-year-old daughter) can be found in the workplace. They don't despise the notion of work; they just aren't as enamored with it as you and I have been taught to be. While we feel a sense of pride after putting in "full day's work for a full day's pay," they simply feel tired.

Unlike you and me, they don't see any correlation between what they do and who they are. They refuse to be defined by their job title or by the quality of their work. To them, work is simply a thing they have to do to get the stuff they want. If they can put in a minimal effort and still get that stuff, then doing more than the minimum is a waste.

I graduated from a suburban, middle-class high school in the 1970s. About half of my closest friends decided not to go on to college but instead jumped right into the workforce and learned a trade. I'll never forget hearing my locker partner describe his plans after graduation. "I just want to get on with a good company that has benefits and rise through the ranks, maybe get into management someday," Ronny said. Thirty years later, he's still working with the post office. Another class-mate took a job as a driver with Pepsi. Today, he's a route supervisor in the Denver bottling plant of PepsiCo.

Free Agent Mentality

Today's youth have no such illusions. Many of their parents have been outsourced, rightsized, and downsized by companies they spent their lives trying to build. Consequently, they've been cautioned about falling into the same trap. They don't buy into "work here 40 years and retire with a gold watch," so you won't hear many talking about long-term em-ployment. Instead, the free agent mentality is practically encoded in their DNA: they want to get as much as they can in exchange for as little as possible. Well, that's an effective way to come out on top—at a garage sale. It certainly doesn't play well on the front lines of your business.

Tap into This Talent

More than anything else, the new work ethic drives managers ab-solutely bonkers. You think, "They don't give a damn!" and complain to friends and colleagues about their lack of effort and commitment. You wonder why they aren't as motivated or *driven* as you were at their age. You see their amazing potential, envy their ability to absorb new infor-mation so quickly, and know they have the technosavvy to create awe-some results—but you might have no idea how to tap into all of this talent. An operations manager for a chain of video stores described it to me this way: "It's like driving a Ferrari on the Autobahn and being stuck in first gear."

4

THE "GIVE A DAMN" CONTINUUM

I previously confessed that, as a 15-year-old boy, I executed a plan that effectively put my employer out of business for an entire evening. Actually, this was not my intent. I knew that Mr. Wong would be angry when he found the sign, but I thought it would just slow down the Friday rush, not end it. I never considered that my prank would totally stop customers from dining there that evening and that Wong would lose a huge percentage of his weekly revenue. Clearly, my intent and the impending result weren't the same.

MINDSET OF DISGRUNTLED EMPLOYEES

Ironically, looking back on this incident with remorse helps me understand the mindset of disgruntled young employees. The first question to answer is this: what does a disgruntled employee look like?

I'm certain that Mr. Wong had no idea that I could, or would, do such a thing. After all, I was a neatly dressed, smiling, polite lad who consistently showed up on time and always sought to please his boss. I never complained, fired a snotty comeback, or even rolled my eyes. Still, trouble was brewing under the cover of my pleasant, respectful demeanor, because Wong showed zero interest in learning how I felt about my job or the way I was treated.

Two Wrongs Don't Make It Right

Regardless of when you grew up or what level of work ethic you were raised with, amazingly you have the potential (though I hope not the inclination) to sabotage your place of employment. It's a safe bet that you've encountered your share of jobs you didn't like and bosses you liked even less, perhaps even loathed. Like me, you can recall times in your past when you've done something to extract revenge on a boss or an organization you felt had wronged you.

Maybe you falsely called in sick, took office supplies for personal use, borrowed unauthorized sample goods and "forgot" to tell anyone about them, made personal long distance calls and logged them as business calls, or appeared productive when you were really doing nothing and getting paid for it.

Sure, some misdeeds occurred with no ill will on your part. What about those times, however, when you intentionally sought to get back at a boss or a company and rationalized your actions, saying, "They don't appreciate my hard work," or, "They owe me," or, "I'll get them!"

I certainly put employee sabotage on the opposite side of the spectrum from supreme commitment, or what I call "total buy in."

NOT AS INVESTED AS YOUR BOSS

If you can get fired from your job, you can't give as much of a damn about your organization as the person who owns the place and could fire you. How could you? It's not your baby. Even if you're a stockholder and give a damn about how your company performs, at least more than non-stockholders, you're still not as invested as those above you on the organizational chart or those who own more stock than you.

As for me, I have total buy in where I work. I would never do anything that would intentionally hurt my employer or cause any degree of difficulty to the company I work for. You see, I own the company I work for and, as the owner, doing anything that would purposely damage my company would equate to career suicide.

At 15, I deliberately sought to put my employer in jeopardy, and today I'll stop at nothing to ensure the unparalleled success of my employer. I've experienced the two

> Here's the truth: Unless you're the owner and/or ultimate decision maker of the organization that employs you, you don't have total buy in.

completely opposite ends of the commitment spectrum, what I call the "give a damn (GAD) continuum."

Give a Damn from Zero to Ten

From sabotage to total buy in, the two end points on the GAD Continuum are as far from each other as east from west. If you don't own 100 percent of the company where you work, you fall somewhere between those two points—and so do your 16- to 24-year-old front-liners.

Using a scale from zero to ten, let's take a look at the GAD Continuum.

0 — 1 — 2 — 3 — 4 — 5 — 6 — 7 — 8 — 9 — 10

Sabotage   Total Buy In

0: Saboteurs. The most commonly used ranking scales run from one to ten. However, if employees feel so angry or disgruntled that they'll try to take the boss or company down, they don't even warrant a one on this scale. For saboteurs, simply quitting the job fails to soothe their wounds; they often want to make a statement and depart in a blaze of ignominious glory. They might opt to engage in stealthy mischief or do something overt to earn bragging rights among their peers.

Many managers secretly fear having a saboteur on their payroll and not knowing it. Any front-liner at the far left end of the GAD Continuum is obviously a workplace hazard, like a virus seeking an opportunity to unleash itself in your computer's hard drive.

Your task: Root out and eliminate saboteurs at all costs.

1 to 3: Disenfranchised employees. These employees won't go out of their way to ruin anything. To do so would take effort and energy and, frankly my dear, they don't give a damn. If your building caught fire, they couldn't even be counted on to pull the alarm.

They don't necessarily hate their jobs; they simply don't feel attached to them and certainly have no buy in. You're not in danger of having disenfranchised employees purposely put you out of business, but they're likely to take a nonchalant attitude that could sure mess things up.

Occasionally, a disenfranchised employee resembles the class clown. You're likely to catch them horsing around on company time when they think supervisors aren't watching. Their actions could even pose a safety risk. If the opportunity presents itself, they'll goof off by pretending to serve customers while actually attempting to make a coworker laugh at how they *don't* serve them.

Generally speaking, disenfranchised workers look for the path of least resistance with little regard for the right way to do something. When questioned, they'll try to make the job look harder than it is, and they won't own up to their own mistakes. They may even take credit for things that others did. In casual conversation, they exaggerate their accomplishments and tell incredible tales, leaving you to discount half of what's said to understand the truth.

If you're tuned in to your workforce, disenfranchised kidployees aren't hard to detect. They are, however, hard to communicate with, difficult to motivate, and impossible to get to perform well in teams.

Your task: Identify and replace them at once.

4 to 6: Bread-and-Butter (B&B) employees. Most employees fall into this category; they represent the big loop area under the bell curve. These kidployees regard work as "just a job" and do what they can to make their bosses happy and company successful, providing the effort doesn't tax them too much. They come to work prepared to do the "minimum daily requirement" (MDR) to get their weekly paychecks. That alone, in fact, becomes their goal.

B&B workers can be extremely bright and talented but unmotivated. Perhaps no one has ever taken the time to show them how to work or explained that each job prepares them for the next. When it comes to success, they don't know what it looks like, they don't believe they are capable of it, or they haven't figured out what it takes to achieve it. In short, they need to be mentored and molded.

Bread-and-butter types, due largely to their prevalence, can make or break your company. They have the ability to move up the continuum if they are led to do so. With coaching, they can make incredible strides. But left unnoticed, unattended, or unappreciated, they can easily slip into a disenfranchised state and create problems.

Your task: Light a fire underneath their raw talent and develop it fully.

7 to 8: Solid subordinates. These folks are among your top-achieving employees. They'll go the extra mile to put a smile on the face of their employer and satisfy even the most discriminating customer. Dependable and responsible, they make a favorable impression on the outside world. In addition, they can be taken at their word and trusted to make good decisions. Solid front-liners know how the game of business is played and have taken the time to learn how your business works from soup to nuts.

Solid kidployees tend to be goal-oriented achievers, and although they might be students studying a totally different field, they know this job counts in the big picture of life. They might have designs on owning or managing a business like yours. At the least, they hope to receive a glowing letter of recommendation from you for their files when they move on to greener pastures.

Your task: Recognize these special people and never take them for granted.

9: Gems. These are the elusive breed of kidployees who are extremely hard to find. Cut them, and they bleed your company colors. They lie awake at night thinking of ways to solve your biggest problems and make your company more profitable. These kidployees don't need to be managed; they require little direction and almost no motivation. Determined to rise from the stockroom to the boardroom, they envision themselves as the future CEO of your company. If you have one of these on your payroll, odds are they are related to the owner—or to Donald Trump.

If you happen to have hit the lottery and have a few Gems on your staff, make them your apprentices and give them special treatment—letting them define what *special* means. Go out of your way to help Gems advance, which is their only goal. If you don't, ultimately they'll find employers who will, leaving you to clutch your kid's Sponge Bob Squarepants pillow in the dark of night lamenting, "God, where did I go wrong?"

Your task: Pull out all stops to retain them. If you can, clone them.

10: Total Buy In. Not an employee, this is the owner or majority stockholder who simply can't turn off the business problem solving at home because it's too much a part of themselves. Stop dreaming. You'll never have an employee at this level, so don't expect it.

Your task: Become a ten yourself, or at least model ten attributes for the benefit of those you employ.

HOW CAN YOU TELL?

As you can see, *buy in* and *giving a damn* are interchangeable terms. When employees have buy in, they give a damn; it would be impossible to have/do one and not the other.

Personal Vested Interest

You want your people to work for you as they would work for their own companies. This only happens if they feel a direct connection to the outcomes created by each and every transaction. For example, salespeople paid a straight commission have a vested interest in every sale, because they get compensated in direct proportion to the amount of the sale. Moreover, they want their customers to become delighted advocates of their products or services so they'll refer their friends. They are concerned about the quality of what they represent, knowing that its quality (or lack of it) directly affects them. By contrast, hourly employees don't automatically feel vested, because their compensation doesn't directly tie to the ups and downs of the enterprise.

> **Buy in** is the degree of an employee's personal vested interest in the image, profits, and long-term success of the organization they work for.

Image

Kidployees who buy in will spot a gum wrapper outside the entrance of your store and pick it up. It's not part of their job description, and maybe they haven't even punched in yet, but they care enough about the business to maintain its curbside appearance. They put the same level of care into sweeping the front lobby and cleaning the bathrooms, realizing how these activities reflect on the business as whole. Teens who buy in might prefer to listen to rap music, but they won't change your radio to their favorite station for fear of alienating prospective patrons. And even if their friends might razz them, kidployees who buy in wear the company uniform and groom themselves as pictured in the employee handbook without any personal alterations or modifications.

Profits

Kidployees who buy in go out of their way to make their employer as profitable as possible. They seek to increase revenues by ensuring quality products and providing great service. If they work at the point of purchase, they enthusiastically suggest additional items to increase the net value of the sale. Further, these young people understand that waste will eat away at the bottom line, so they go out of their way to avoid unnecessary use of resources and vigilantly guard the inventory against shrinkage.

Long-Term Success

Kidployees who buy in operate (to the best of their ability and understanding) much like owner of the company.

As an owner/manager/supervisor, you're aware of the connection between what happens today and the effect down the road. You could generate instant sales by manipulating the customer or making ridiculous price reductions, but the long-term impact of those decisions would likely prove fatal to your business. Kidployees who buy in to their jobs take this knowledge to heart, wanting to ensure that their company has a future that's as bright as the one they hope to have for themselves. As much as they want to please you by making a sale today, they won't mislead the customer just to close a quick deal, and they won't give away merchandise just to get rid of an unhappy camper. Although they realize their future with the company might be limited, they want it to be around when their kids look for work someday. They make decisions accordingly.

It's Not Who They Are, It's Where They're At

The GAD continuum isn't about permanently assigning a number to a person but rather determining where certain employees stand at a specific point in time. It helps you recognize their true potential, so you can assist them in moving up on the scale for everyone's benefit.

You and I could independently observe the same front-line employee at work for a few hours. Then, after a brief interview, we could assess that employee's buy in and both assign the same number or close to it (for example, maybe Jennifer's buy in is four and Thad's is six). Remember, an employee's GAD rating can move up and down on the continuum; it's not etched in stone. It's simply used to assess where individuals rate with respect to how much they currently give a damn about their jobs.

Coming in Lower

Your front-liners likely rate lower than you do on the GAD continuum. (If not, perhaps you should report to them!) Likewise, the front-liners who are hard-to-understand kidployees rate lower on the GAD continuum than 16- to 24-year-olds of previous eras.

Times most assuredly have changed. As discussed earlier, parents and teachers rarely focus the importance of GAD before young people enter the workforce. As such, most of your front-liners come into your employ at a ranking between three and five, compared to your probable rating between five and seven when you entered the workforce at the same age.

Take note: That doesn't mean this world is completely void of eager-beaver young teens determined to set the world on fire. This kind of worker, however, is in shorter supply today than before.

Every Player Matters

Today, businesses have the equipment and technology to complete many key functions that, a decade or more ago, had to be handled manually. However, even though the young people on your payroll feel impatient completing transactions that can't be handled by a machine, you still depend on them to do so. Interestingly, the typical kidployee today generates a significantly higher sales yield than their counterpart a generation ago. Hence, each front-line employee is crucial to your success; you have little room on your payroll for anyone who doesn't rate a five or above on the GAD continuum.

YOUR MISSION, SHOULD YOU CHOOSE TO ACCEPT IT

As a business owner or manager, you obviously want to hire kidployees who will show up from day one with the highest possible level of buy in and rate high on the GAD continuum. Your job flows more easily when you have gung-ho kidployees ready, willing, and able to be molded into Gems. Even when your operation is fully staffed, you'll always make room for a Gem.

On the flip side, perhaps you've hired kids thinking they rated a seven only to find out they rated a four. Worse, perhaps you're new to your position and have inherited a staff laden with disenfranchised kidployees who are costing money and driving away customers. This makes you wonder if it's worth the hassle to clean house and start from scratch, or if you can turn things around by playing the employee hand you've been dealt.

Inspire Positive Change

A tugboat doesn't remain with a barge throughout its entire destination; it simply takes the vessel out to open waters and sets it on the correct course. Like that tugboat, you can significantly alter the course of your entire business by directing your front-liners and nudging them on their way.

Just remember that you are a leader, and leadership is about inspiring positive change among your troops. Anyone can achieve great results with an army of Gems, while managing Solid Subordinates is no great trick because they perform well even when unsupervised. Clearly, sustaining a great business means being able to nudge lower-rated kidployees from where they are to where they could be—to nudge a four into a five, and a six into a seven or eight.

Happily, if your front line is populated by those rated five through eight, you can create an environment of positive influences that draw threes and fours upward. In a self-sustaining environment, the Disenfranchised stand out if they don't toe the line. Their lack of buy in then becomes an ankle weight, and no kid wants to be seen as the unworthy exception.

Easier Said Than Done

To be a successful employer of young talent, work diligently to recognize that talent, attract it, and most importantly, develop it. Easier said than done, I know. However, if you can inspire every kidployee who works for you to move upward on the GAD scale, the results will astound you.

Remember, you won't get anyone—and certainly not a perceptive, streetwise kidployee—to buy in to your operation at any point on the GAD continuum greater than where you rate yourself. So, if your success depends on their buy in, you have to

- be *personally invested* to a greater degree than they are.
- sacrifice yourself to the *image* to a greater degree than you expect them to do.
- strive to *produce more* and *waste less* than they do.
- continually show that you want to foster success for your organization over the *long term.*

HOW TO
ATTRACT THEM

The Quickest Way to Get Them
to Give a Damn Is to Start
with Those Who Do

5

THE OPIE IDEAL

Before he was a famous director of such Hollywood blockbusters as *Backdraft, Apollo 13, Ransom,* and *A Beautiful Mind,* Ron Howard starred in a TV show called *Happy Days.* But I grew up with a younger Ronny Howard in the role of Opie, the son of the town sheriff on *The Andy Griffith Show.* First airing in black and white in 1960, *The Andy Griffith Show* broadcasts in syndication to this day and is on record as one of the most watched television programs in history. Reflecting the cultural values of its time, Opie's character has been deeply woven into the American cultural fabric.

On the TV show, Opie is Andy's only son and his pride and joy. To Andy, Opie is more important than his role as sheriff, than the women he dates, and than anything else in his life. Each episode, the father-son tandem has involved discussions in which Opie learns valuable lessons that mold his character.

Fast forward to 1968, when young Opie has matured into a teen. He wants a new guitar to play in a rock band, but Andy isn't about to run out and buy one for his son. Instead, he tells Opie that he's old enough to earn his own spending money.

Opie sees a *Help Wanted* sign in the window of the corner drug store, enters, and applies for a job as a soda jerk. The owner, Mr. Crawford, isn't keen on hiring a teenager, but he knows that Opie comes from a fine home and has a good reputation, so he decides to take a chance.

With some nervousness, he hires this clean-cut and enthusiastic young lad.

To Mr. Crawford's delight, Opie turns out to be an ideal part-time employee from day one. He wears his clean white apron with pride and tilts his soda fountain hat with style and confidence. The poster boy of responsibility, Opie is punctual, ambitious, respectful, polite, cheerful, honest, and eager to please.

Tragedy Strikes!

One afternoon during a quiet time, Opie accidentally strikes a bottle of expensive perfume with his broomstick handle while sweeping the floor. The glass bottle shatters. He worries that this accident will get him fired and that his pa will be disappointed and embarrassed. Working alone when the incident occurs, Opie could easily deny any involvement or even concoct a story that would get him off the hook. But instead, Opie uses his entire first week's paycheck to purchase another bottle of perfume via mail order. He replaces the broken bottle with the new one and goes back to work. But then Mr. Crawford accidentally knocks the bottle off the shelf. Instead of getting upset, he shrugs it off and tells Opie that it's no big deal because it's a display tester, filled only with colored water.

Then Opie confesses his blunder, telling Mr. Crawford that he knocked the bottle off and, thinking it was the real thing, used his own money to replace it. Although Mr. Crawford discovers he had just broken a real bottle, he praises Opie for his honesty and Andy's chest swells with pride. As usual in Mayberry, everyone lives happily ever after.

Wishful Recollection

Watching (or hearing about) that episode, we might say to ourselves, "Doggone it, I was a lot like Opie when I got my first job." Although we probably didn't measure up to Opie's fictional example, it comforts us to think we did. If you remember not being anything like Opie in your first job (you behaved more like I did at the Pagoda Restaurant) but could step into a time machine and go back to your first job and try it again, I bet you'd emulate him. Why? Because from a mature vantage point, we've seen firsthand how far the Opies in this world go; they almost always wind up on top.

Frankly, how you and I approached jobs in our teens and early 20s isn't the issue. Today, we've assumed the role of Mr. Crawford, and we're nervous about entrusting our operations to inexperienced young help. Knowing that it's inevitable, we at least want the kids we employ to be responsible, respectful, cheerful, and eager to please, as Opie was. We're looking for kidployees who show up on time, wear proper apparel, and sprint down the street to get errands done then sprint back to work. Further, we want kidployees who are honest to a fault. We want Opie.

> The good news is that Opies are out there, even today. The bad news is that they're exceedingly hard to find and even harder to hang on to.

Back then, an employer could reasonably expect a sizeable percentage of applicants to be Opies. The Disenfranchised kidployee was a rare breed and Saboteurs even rarer. Today the tables have turned. Disenfranchised kids are much more common, and the number of Saboteurs appears to be on the rise. This might leave you scratching your head, wondering when Opie will see the sign in your window and come in to apply.

OPIE'S CLEVER DISGUISE

As kids, we grew up with *The Andy Griffith Show* and saw Opie as a role model. We watched how he approached his drugstore job, liked him for his goodness, and saw that he somehow always wound up smiling in the end. We certainly didn't think of Opie as a nerd, a dork, or a kiss-ass. The youth of today wouldn't be so kind. Opie would be pegged as all of the above and a sell-out to boot. He would be seen as a dork or a dweeb whom no one wants to be like.

This doesn't mean that Opie is extinct, only that he's not walking around with a short red hair and a freckle-faced smile. The Opie that comes into your store likely flies below your radar. He might be wearing baggy jeans and have a tattoo, or she might show her midriff and sport a naval ring. But if you pass them off as "one of *those*," you could be letting a Gem slip away.

A lot of awesome kids with Opie-esque qualities are looking for work and eagerly want to exceed their boss' expectations. In spite of their age and a pop culture that fights it, these young prospects recognize that doing their best on a job complements their overall career path, personal development, and life trajectory. They're searching for a meaningful employment experience; as long as they feel as though they're learning and serving, it doesn't much matter whether they're scooping ice cream or entering data in a computer.

An Encounter with a Modern Day Opie

Not long ago, I walked into a Wal-Mart just minutes before closing time in a panic to buy a small tape recorder for an important project that wouldn't wait until morning. All the employees were scurrying to close their registers and go home. The managers were flickering the lights and making announcements over the intercom to hurry the straggling shoppers. I sprinted to the electronics counter and asked the young kidployee named Matt (who had long disheveled hair and a scruffy beard) if he would point me in the direction of the tape recorders. "Sure thing, sir. Follow me," he said politely and enthusiastically. He stopped what he was doing and took me three aisles away. "We have a really good Sony that's on sale," Matt said. Acting as if he were totally oblivious to the lateness of the hour, he carefully took the recorder out of the package, put it in my hand, and begin pointing out its cool features. "Will this one do the trick for you, or would you like to see what else we have?" he asked. I told him the Sony would work great. Then he walked me to the next aisle saying, "Better make certain you've got fresh batteries and blank tapes, or the recorder won't do you much good." He looked about 17, but he must have been Sam Walton incarnate!

Even though Matt was a part-time, hourly employee who didn't stand to gain a nickel in the transaction—and I was the only thing standing in the way of his punching out—he treated me as if we were at Matt-Mart and I was buying a dozen big-screen TVs. Charm, grace, manners, knowledge, enthusiasm—this kid had the full deck.

You see, Opies instinctively recognize that business is a transactional affair. In each customer encounter, their overriding objective is to ensure their customers get what they came for and leave delighted. An Opie working in a supermarket doesn't simply say, "I think the muffin mix is in aisle three." She takes you there and makes sure it's the brand you're looking for. An Opie at the deli counter won't merely take your order. He'll double check it to make certain the cook prepared it correctly before handing it to you. Opies in high tech don't feel the need to impress you with their product knowledge, nor do they attempt to overwhelm you with features you'll never use. Instead, they find out about your specific needs and address them in a way that makes sense to you without coming off as condescending.

Opies are confident without being cocky. They don't fish for compliments, because they know they're doing a good job. When it appears they've satisfied their customers, they go the extra mile to cart your goods to the register, make sure the cashier rings up the discounted sales price, and get help taking your merchandise to your car.

Opies have a photographic memory, or at least it appears that they do. When you return to the store, they might not approach you with a "Hi, Mr. Chester!" but at least they'll give you a friendly nod and a smile, letting you know that you're important to them. They might even refer to your earlier purchase, saying something like, "Hey, how did that tape recorder work out for you?"

Opies genuinely care how their stores look, how their products work, and how their brand is perceived. They enjoy interacting with customers and feel good when they know they've helped solve a problem.

How Do You Know When Opies Are Present?

- They smile, radiating warmth and enthusiasm.
- They look you in the eye.
- They firmly shake your hand.
- They never say unkind things about other people, products, or competitors.
- They are honest; they won't stretch the truth.
- They are professionally modest.
- They speak clearly and distinctively; they use acceptable grammar.
- They let you speak first and last and don't hog the conversation.
- They listen to you and value your opinion.
- They deal in common courtesies and say, "Yes, sir," and, "No, ma'am."
- They have an unmistakable confirming presence, showing confidence without cockiness and acting friendly without being familiar.
- They're not merely eager to please; they're *determined* to please.
- They show respect and don't assume they can call you by your first name or casual label; e.g., "Yeah, man," "Sure thing, sweetheart," or "Okay, buddy."

6

IDENTIFYING OPIES

f you think Opie is a myth—a product of a bygone era—then skip this chapter, because there's simply no way you'd be able to attract an Opie into your business. And you certainly wouldn't retain him if you believe he no longer exists.

But I know from firsthand experience that a lot of Opies are out there. I run across them at student leadership conferences, high school assemblies, college campuses, and church youth groups. I encounter them at coffee shops, burger joints, mall kiosks, and on the other end of the phone line. Recently, I met one at Wal-Mart.

This doesn't mean, however, that Matt (the Opie I met at Wal-Mart) would be a great kidployee in your organization. Even if I saw Matt continue to shine over a series of transactions, even if his supervisor gave him a glowing review, even if Matt came to live with me for a year and I came to believe he's the greatest kid the world has ever known, I still couldn't say he'd be the right kidployee for you. How could I, unless I knew as much about you and your business as I did about Matt?

FINDING THE RIGHT OPIE

A master carpenter uses the right tool for each specific job. He might own one expensive, awesome tool among many average ones, but the world's finest hammer won't saw a two-by-four in half, and a titanium gold-plated saw with a lifetime guarantee isn't going to drive a nail through a wall.

As told in the movie *Miracle,* the 1980 U.S. Olympic hockey team shocked the world by defeating the heavily favored Soviet Union team and going on to capture the gold medal. In the film, Kurt Russell played the part of Herb Brooks, the team's coach, whose job began with assembling a team from a large pool of amateur college players.

In an early scene, Herb's assistant coach, Craig Patrick, noticed Coach Brooks crossing out the names of some of the best players—the most physically gifted or skilled ones. Alarmed, Patrick said, "Herb, you're cutting the best players!" Coach Brooks replied, "I'm not looking for the *best* players; I'm looking for the *right* players."

Don't Confuse *Best* with *Right*

It's easy to fall into the trap of narrowing your search for Opie to the best student, the best athlete, the best-looking kid you can find. We might be impressed when we have a chance to hire the captain of the football team or the cheerleading squad, the student body president, the editor of the school paper, or the lead in the school play. But demonstrated excellence in one or more of these areas doesn't always translate to excellence on the job.

Some kids are born with great physical skills, many are artistic by nature, and others are brilliant in the classroom. Certain kids find work to be their "thing." Although they don't excel in school-related activities, they're destined for greatness in the world of work. And although I don't know him personally, I would guess that Matt fits this stereotype. I know that I did at his age.

While it's good to look for leadership qualities in your young talent and give special consideration to kids already active in worthy pursuits, putting an overachieving, totally involved student on your payroll could actually come back to haunt you. After all, between school, friends, and a schedule packed with practices, games, and studying, when would they manage to squeeze in their jobs?

Opie is not an absolute term; it's situational. A person who's an Opie for you might not be Opie for another manager. If you're in the service business, for example, you're looking for a different kind of kidployee than somebody in manufacturing.

PROFILING: NOT AN EXACT SCIENCE BUT IT HELPS

To attract an Opie into your business, first get to know what an Opie in your business looks like. In the previous chapter, we discussed the common traits of an Opie, including the one at Wal-Mart. But although Matt behaves like Opie in the electronics department, he might be a completely different kind of employee in the shoe department or behind the snack counter. Aside from being a well-mannered, polite kid, Matt is obviously passionate about electronics. He wouldn't morph into a rude, arrogant, in-your-face kidployee if he took a job at Burger King, but his GAD might be reduced to something left of a six.

What constitutes an Opie in your business?

Shopping for Cars

As a Depression-era baby, my dad compulsively shopped for bargains and demanded a deal every time money was exchanged. For example, he wanted to make certain I got the best deal when I bought my first car. But to him, the only thing that mattered was price. So what could have been an enjoyable father-son bonding experience ultimately became a futile exercise in mental gymnastics with lots of screaming and shouting.

The ordeal began when we opened the massive Sunday paper, turned to the automobile classifieds, and started scanning the thousands of listings. From Audis to Volvos, anything within $500 of what I had saved was circled. Dad had me call on anything and everything that seemed remotely affordable, whether or not I liked it. "Here's a Corvette without an engine. You could take auto shop at school and learn how to put one in." Then a minute later, he'd say, "Oh, here's an ad for an old hearse. It might be a little creepy, but you could take a lot of your friends up to the mountains skiing!" I honestly didn't know whether I'd end up with a moped or a school bus, but I quickly discovered how hard it was to find something when you didn't know what that "something" was.

As a father to four kids today, I assume the role of helping each of them find used cars while refusing to put them through the same agony my dad put me through. So before the search begins, I instruct them to create a written profile of what they think they're looking for. I ask them to list the reasons they need a car and state how it will be used: "I need something to haul my band equipment around," "I want to get a job delivering pizzas," and so on. I also ask them to write down what they *don't* want: "Nothing that has more than 100,000 miles on it," or, "I hate lime green," and so on. We then discuss the type of vehicle (truck, economy car, front-wheel drive, etc.) that will meet their written objectives. Next, we identify the brands and models that would most likely meet their needs and be affordable. Only after they lay out this profile do they open the local newspaper or hit the Internet. Within a matter of minutes, they're able to circle half a dozen dead-on possibilities.

Shopping for Kidployees

How do you create a similar profile at work? Start by considering those who have been Opies for you in the past—after all, success leaves clues. What characteristics of Jose, Nikki, and Sarah set them apart from the others? Conversely, why did Jarrod quit after only three weeks, and why did Kara fizzle after such a strong start? Solicit input from the direct supervisors of your front-line staff. Identify the top achievers as well as those who struggled; list the Gems and the Disenfranchised. Search for the common denominators by asking these kinds of questions:

- What kind of students are they?
- In what subjects do they excel?
- What kinds of activities and interests do they have outside of school?
- What kind of home or family do they come from?
- Do they volunteer for any type of community service?
- What do they do with the money they earn?
- How would you characterize their closest friends?
- What is their driving record like?
- How do they respond when asked, "What does the future hold for you?"
- What are their preferences for movies, music, and television programs?

Some of the information gleaned from these questions can be pulled from an application or résumé, while some cannot. In fact, employment laws may prohibit you from asking employees some of these questions due to matters of privacy or discrimination, but that doesn't mean the answers aren't easily available. Through casual conversation and obser-vation, you can learn a great deal about the young people on your pay-roll and what it takes to succeed in your company.

A number of companies have spent considerable time determining the personality traits of their Opies. To identify the red flags that identify a candidate who isn't a good fit, they use assessment tools that applicants complete as a condition of consideration. This kind of profiling, although not an exact science, enables employers to more easily separate the Opies from the non-Opies among their applicants.

Let's examine how this approach has worked in practice.

Case Study

ROCK SOLID APPLICANTS

Rock Bottom Brewery (the parent company for Old Chicago and Chop House restaurants) doesn't like to roll the dice and gamble with its hired help. Its managers have carefully identified the attributes and traits of their best employees by position (greeters, bartenders, servers, cooks, etc.) and have a good idea what an Opie in each of these positions looks like. Using this information, they've created an online assessment that's become an integral part of their application process to help determine which applicants possess the attitudes, skills, and behaviors that are commonplace among their top achievers.

It takes 40 minutes to complete the application—that's the downside. The upside is that the company really knows applicants before hiring them, thus greatly reducing unwanted surprise factors and adding to its database of key traits. If a hired hand turns out to be an Opie, Rock Bottom can refer back to that person's application and assessment to gain an even deeper insight into the qualities needed for success in their environment.

Case Study

THE DOMINO EFFECT

Around 1991, the tractor-trailer drivers who supplied all of the Domino's pizza stores nationwide collectively earned the top annual award for safety from the National Highway Transportation Safety Association. This group of drivers had the fewest traffic citations and logged the most miles of accident-free driving.

It stands to reason that the best among all the Domino's truck drivers—the company that had won the national award for safe driving—would be among the best commercial drivers in the country. But when questioned, the vice president of Domino's Pizza Distribution Company didn't know the name of this individual or the names of any of the company's top-ten drivers.

Domino's decided to start identifying its top performers. As they gathered the information, the managers recognized and rewarded the best. The upper executives got to know them by name and meet them. Once they began to assess the traits and habits of their best drivers, they applied that data and sought others who matched the profile.

I LIKE THIS PLACE

The more kidployees like working at a place, the less likely they care about the amount of their pay. The right kidployees feel at home in your environment; leaving your business would be like running away from home.

An Expert in Every Department

Dick's Sporting Goods, with huge stores across the country, offers kidployees a standard wage. Nevertheless, working there is attractive to them because of the positions available. The company actively seeks young athletes to represent various departments within their stores. In the golf department, you'd find a kidployee who loves golf, plays for his high school team, and talks about Tiger Woods all day. In the outdoor recreation department, you'd find kidployees who like to camp and explore. They'd not only tell you what kind of tent to buy, but they'd explain the best places to go for the weekend.

Barnes & Noble actively seeks kidployees who love to read, especially those with a broad-based knowledge of literature or the classics. To nurture a specific type of culture, this company wants studious kidployees who look clean-cut and have the instincts of a librarian.

A kidployee who feels at home at Barnes & Noble might act like a fish out of water at Borders, and vice versa. The comfort factor is certainly in the mind of the beholder. But kidployees will likely stay in a work environment where they learn and feel recognized for the good things they do—where they feel most comfortable.

Its biggest competitor takes a completely different approach to staffing. Border's Books prefers to hire experts by topic, much the same way Dick's Sporting Goods does. In the computer book section, for example, you're apt to find young geeks who spend every cent they earn on technogadgetry, while in children's books, you'd be helped by a college student majoring in elementary education. Borders is less concerned about a kidployee's personal appearance than Barnes & Noble; its managers understand that the right kidployee for the music department might come equipped with a lip ring and green hair.

It's a Jungle Out There

Be assured, a lot of Opies in your vicinity want to give a damn about your business and your customers. They're chomping at the bit to put their skills and abilities to work for you. However, the trick is finding them and attracting them to your business—before your competitor snatches them up.

This isn't easy. It takes time and money to develop a reliable method of identifying the potential Gems and red-flagging the Disenfranchised. But when you realize the dramatic effect the wrong fit can have on your bottom-line profits, you regard it as an investment that will pay huge dividends.

RECRUITING OPIES

The easiest way to find your Opies is to make it easy for them to find you—to throw out your net and hope they get caught in it.

Bait your pole, lodge it between two rocks, go back to what you were doing, and wait until you hook a winner. After all, if you just do as Mr. Crawford did and put a *Help Wanted* sign in your window, your Opies will come running in, right?

Well, in an age when the supply of Opies exceeded the demand for their services, this worked like a charm. But that was then, and this is now. You're not in Mayberry, and Mr. Crawford's corner drug has been replaced by a Walgreen's.

ATTRACT AND HIRE THE RIGHT PEOPLE

Ninety-five percent of the personnel problems you face can be eliminated by recruiting the right people into your company or organization. If you're spending a disproportionate amount of your time on the hire-fire-hire-fire treadmill and thinking, "That's just the way it is with these flaky kids today," you haven't figured out how to attract and hire the right ones for your business.

Make no mistake: the Gems are out there to be attracted. The irony is, they want to work for you as badly as you want them in your employ. One of you has to seek out the other. With young talent in such short supply, you're competing with businesses of every size and kind—not just with those in your own industry. Because every employer wants to hire Opie, the odds of his waltzing into your store to fill out an application without being enticed or prompted are slim.

In any given locale, only a small percentage of kidployee prospects will be Opies. That's why whenever we encounter them, we're forced to do a double take. What's my evidence? A customer in 1954, 1964, or even 1984 wouldn't have been surprised by the kind of service I got from Matt at Wal-Mart; they would have expected it. Would you today?

Tilt Percentages in Your Favor

In the new millennium, successful employers subscribe to the Law of Large Numbers. This law demands that you are constantly recruiting, constantly interviewing, and constantly looking for ways to increase your applicant flow, even when you're fully staffed. It's foolish to post signs that state *Not Accepting Applications;* your entire employment situation can change overnight. And if you get caught with your cupboards bare, you're toast.

When I ask managers what percentage of kidployee job candidates in their communities are Opies, most reply "about 10 percent." Assuming this is true all over, that means only one out of every ten applicants is a sure thing. So, if you want to hire 10 "sure things," you need to screen a minimum of 100 applicants and hope you can land the prized number. Unfortunately, an application submitted by an Opie two weeks ago is about as good as those you have on file from 1982. That Opie is already working for your competitor.

> Recruiting Opie is not an event; it's a perpetual process. You've got to outthink, outmaneuver, and outrecruit your competitors, if you want to hire the best and the brightest. Don't let the Opies right in front of you get away.

SIGN UP THE EASY CATCHES

Just because posting a sign in search of help is old-fashioned doesn't mean that it won't occasionally land you an Opie. Let the world around you know you're in the market for young talent, because even if the per-

son who spics your posting isn't a candidate, they probably know someone who is. This is also a low-cost way to advertise a job opening. But for
crying out loud, don't do a "Mr. Crawford" and post a two-dollar, red-
and-white *Help Wanted* sign from the local hardware store. If you want to
catch the eye of an Opie, go the extra mile.

- **Be fresh.** *Help Wanted, Now Accepting Job Applications,* and *Now Hiring* phraseology is so yesterday. Show that you're in step with the
  times and use phrases like *Our Team Is Growing; Grow With Us, Sport
  Our Colors—and Get Paid for It!,* and *Only the Best and Brightest Need
  Apply.* Tokyo Joes, a small chain of quick-service eateries in Colorado, actually seeks out alternative-edge type kidployees. It announces job openings on a cool tabletop sign that reads, *The Few
  . . . The Proud . . . The Pierced . . . or Whatever!* But don't adopt.
  Adapt. Being fresh means being original. And if you're at a loss
  for the right syntax, solicit ideas from your kidployees!
- **Be different.** Use lots of color and visual imagery on your sign.
  Show photos of your hip-looking kidployees and make certain
  that your brand is recognizable. Don't just hang your masterpiece
  in your front window; duplicate it and post copies in your public
  restrooms, your fitting rooms, and above your water fountains.
  Print your notice on the back of customers' receipts or on your
  bags. Some grocery stores advertise job openings on small signs
  positioned inside the shopping cart. Snowbird Ski Area in Utah
  gives away free logo stickers—always a big hit with teens. On the
  backside of the sticker, the peel-away portion, it says *NOW HIRING*
  and lists the company's job Web site.
- **Be direct.** What exactly do you want your prospects to do when
  they see your sign? *Inquire Within* or *See Manager* isn't effective,
  particularly if the manager isn't available and a prospective young
  Opie approaches the kidployee you want to replace. Give prospects
  an easy-to-remember Web site or a phone number that's answered
  by a person, not voice mail. Make certain to streamline each of
  these processes; you don't want to turn off your best prospects by
  making them jump through too many hoops.

FISH THE STOCKED LAKES

If I want to catch a marlin, I don't fish the stream that runs by my
home in Golden, Colorado. If I'm looking for rainbow trout, I don't go

deep-sea fishing off the coast of Florida. Marlins live in the ocean; trout hang out in mountain streams. Duh.

Fishing for the right kidployee uses the exact same principle. After you create the profile and identify the common denominators discussed in Chapter 5, recruit where your prime candidates are most likely to be—that is, fish the stocked lakes. A manager of a music store fishes for a different kind of kid than the manager of the neighborhood bowling alley. The perfect kidployee for a radiator repair shop would probably quit after one week if he had to work in a bookstore. Although marlins and trout are both fish, they die quickly if they're placed in each other's environment. So do kidployees.

Your Kind of Fish

In the car business, they say, "There's a butt for every seat." In other words, no matter what kind of car is for sale, a buyer is looking for that identical make and model. The trick is to match the two.

In the same way, a number of kids who are floating about your community would make perfect kidployees for your business. They'd love nothing better than to put their talents and passions to work for you. You'd find them easy to train and easy to manage. They'd also come into your employ at seven-plus on the GAD scale from day one. But who are they? Where are they? And what jobs are they biting on?

Frankly, the key to solving your recruiting problems lies in your ability to determine what kind of fish you need and where that kind gathers. Let's say that you operate a restaurant and frequently look to fill positions for host/greeters and wait staff. Because they're on your front lines interacting with your customers, you need young people who are outgoing, friendly, and enthusiastic. After interviewing the best kidployees on your staff and soliciting input from your shift managers, you discover that your best greeters and servers get involved in speech, drama, and music at their respective schools. Eureka! You've just determined where your kind of fish lives.

To fish these lakes, get dialed in to the theater arts departments at various high schools and colleges in your area and begin attending local concerts and plays. It would be in your best interests to become friends—or at least acquaintances—with the drama and choir teachers. You can even offer to host cast parties, donate materials for building sets, and advertise your restaurant in the event programs. Let these people know from the onset that you have an interest in offering part-time employment to energetic students. Agree to schedule work times around their practices and performances. In these ways, you cement your position as the employer of choice among these key prospects.

> Think and act long term if you want to rid yourself of frequent short-term hiring problems.

Fish or Cut Bait

Is recruiting this way worthwhile? After all, it's a hassle and you don't have the time or budget dollars to go through this additional work, right?

Wrong. Weighed against the time and money you spend recruiting, training, and managing kidployees who don't work out because they're the "wrong fish" to begin with, taking steps to find the right streams for the "right fish" can be your best investment of time and resources ever.

C a s e   S t u d y

JOSTENS'S JOCKS

Minneapolis-based Jostens, founded in 1897, provides products, programs, and services that help people celebrate important moments, recognize achievements, and build affiliations. The company's products include yearbooks, class rings, graduation products, school photography, and products for athletic champions and their fans.

Selling directly into high schools, Jostens employs a great many former college and pro athletes to provide sales and service to this niche. Jostens believes that athletes take pride in their schools and appreciate the recognition they receive for their accomplishments. They also know that athletes are used to long hours, hard work, and personal sacrifice—qualities they seek in their associates.

Generally, high school athletes get involved in their school's decision to select a company that will create the official class ring, yearbook, and so on. These students tend to admire adults with noteworthy sports achievements and often look up to them as heroes and role models. Understandably, when a Jostens representative appears on campus, they draw a lot of attention and often bond quickly with students, teachers, and administrators.

When hiring a sales associate, therefore, Jostens knows exactly what kind of fish to look for. It doesn't take a genius to figure out where they focus their recruiting efforts. They've been able to make what could be a hit-and-miss proposition into a relatively simple and painless process, just by knowing which lakes to fish in.

CREATE A PIPELINE TO YOUR FRONT DOOR

What would it be worth for you to spend less time fishing because Opies come in droves seeking employment? They will come if you understand the importance of key alliances.

In the restaurant example, we showed how a manager who had identified the common denominator of his top performers (drama students) could go directly to the source (theater departments of local schools) to recruit potential Gems. With this effort, it wouldn't be long before that restaurant developed a self-perpetuating reputation as the place drama students go to work.

Further, if you were recruiting young sales reps for Jostens, knowing that ex-athletes make great prospects, wouldn't it be wise to your time and resources to form alliances with team coaches?

The lesson here? You don't have to know all the Opies in your community as long as you know the people who know them: interested teachers, coaches, guidance counselors, program sponsors, and others who interact with your best prospects day in and day out.

Guidance counselors especially can readily tell you which students are looking for work. In some situations, it may also be possible for them to share with you a student's academic and attendance records—both possible indicators of how they might perform on the job. Vocational teachers work with students who have demonstrated interest in a specific career and want experience in that particular field. And there is no better judge of kids' work habits and determination than their coaches.

Your community is chock-full of adults like these who love students and want to help them find meaningful experiences. But they are overworked and underpaid; they won't come to you. You won't have much success creating your pipeline if, out of the blue, you phone a local high school guidance counselor and say, "Hello. This is the manager of Shoe World. You know any kid who's looking for a job?" For your pipeline to work, lay it out in advance and take the initiative to formulate a strategic alliance with these key contacts.

> Create a pipeline that brings the right kind of kid directly into your business. Remember, it wasn't raining when Noah built the ark.

YOUR APPLICATION PROCEDURE

You can increase your application flow simply by streamlining your application process. First, make applications easy to find on your Web site. Next, ensure that your employees know how to effectively handle application requests. If the form is long and tedious, revamp it and take out anything that's not absolutely necessary. When possible, use clever jargon and cool language to make it more fun and attractive. Why make your prospects' first impression a boring one?

One of the hippest applications I've seen comes from the huge kid-ployer, Chipotle, the McDonald's-owned quick-serve burrito joint based in Denver. Chipotle not only uses its burrito-based jargon in its marketing but also in its application procedure.

Here are a few excerpts taken from the company's online application form at http://www.chipotle.com.

- *Benefits: salaried employees.* We live to make gourmet burritos, but you need some down time, too. Two weeks a year, but you start earning it from day one. And after three months you can take it. At the beginning of your fifth year, you start earning an extra week of vacation. Part-timers are eligible based on the hours they work.
- *Benefits: hourly employees.* Flexible hours are a way of life at Chipotle. So are biannual merit increases and opportunities for advancement Fiestas. We're closed New Year's, Easter, Fourth of July (not in all our restaurants), Thanksgiving, and Christmas. So restaurant crews get those days off.
- *Peace of mind: salaried employees only.* We offer company-paid benefits for anyone working 32 hours or more per week. All you have to do is sign up when you begin the burrito life. Benefits vary slightly by region. Chipotle pays most of the cost for your medical and dental. Life and short-term disability are paid by Chipotle. We share the cost of coverage for dependents. There are also some

options, like long-term disability and supplemental life insurance, which you can elect to pay for yourself.

- *Smart saving.* A companywide favorite (as long as you're 21—that's the law). After your first month of employment, you can contribute anywhere from 1 to 15 percent of your salary into a 401(k) plan. After a year, Chipotle will match dollar-for-dollar on the first 3 percent of your contributions and 50¢ of every dollar on the next 2 percent of your contributions. And you are immediately vested in both your and Chipotle's contributions, which means all the money saved belongs to you entirely, even if you decide to leave Chipotle.

- *Just in case.* If you need it, you are eligible for five sick days per year (prorated if you only work part of the year). After three months with us, you can use it. Part-timers are eligible based on the hours they work.

- *Lunch, dinner, etc.* You eat free during work. Enough said.

- *Other cool perks: salaried employees.* Bonus, tuition reimbursement, credit union, quality of life, training, direct deposit, company cars, organized companywide events.

- *Other cool perks: hourly employees.* Free T-shirts, referral bonus, quality of life, training, and running with the Big Dogs as we conquer the world one burrito at a time.

- *How to apply.* You can get the three-page Chipotle job application by clicking the link below. This is an Adobe Acrobat Portable Document, so you'll need the Acrobat Reader to open this file. Once you fill out the application, please fax or mail it to us.

    Thanks for wanting to join our Chipotle family. Like you, several others are also interested in joining us. Because of this, it will take us some time to select the most qualified candidates for an interview. If we select you (you lucky dog) for an interview, we will be in touch within a few weeks. We appreciate all your time and effort in submitting your qualifications.

- *Résumé.* If you're ready to let us know how you can help us, send us your résumé. We can accept résumés as either text (no formatting) or in Microsoft Word format. Please send your résumé to wazeehr@chipotle.com. You can also mail or fax your résumé to us. Make sure your cover letter describes the job you're interested in.

- *Working at our headquarters doesn't suck.* We're a young company and growing like a weed—so there's tons of opportunity. Everyone's good at what they do. It's a fast-paced place but also relaxed. Get in. Work hard. Enjoy life. No politics. No suits. Just good people who are most excellent at what they do. Not to mention our cool offices located in Denver's jumpin' LoDo warehouse district. Click around and look for something to do.

Follow-up

Follow-up is critical. When an application comes in, respond immediately—within 24 hours. Get in contact with all applicants, even if it's just a touch-base call or e-mail, to thank them for their interest. Odds are, the person who coined the phrase "if you snooze you lose" was recruiting a kidployee.

Young employees will learn a lot about how your company values customer service by the way their application is processed in the early phases of the hiring process. After all, most kids view getting a job as cold and intimidating, a task requiring mounds of redundant paperwork, sitting in sterile rooms for a battery of tests and interviews, and then having to wait nervously until a person in authority accepts or rejects them. Then, when they get the thumbs up, they're told to make customers feel warmly welcome and pleasantly served. Insanely stupid, if you ask me. Treat your applicants the way you want your employees to treat your vendors, customers, and even superiors.

> Make a concerted effort to make your applicants feel welcomed and appreciated in the early phases and expedite the entire application, interview, and screening process, and you'll soon discover that successful applicants also rate high on the GAD scale.

HOW TO
KEEP THEM

You Simply Can't Afford to Lose
Anyone Who Gives a Damn

8

RETENTION: HANG ON FOR DEAR LIFE

Imagine this. While buying your morning coffee, you inadvertently leave your wallet or purse on the counter. Several hours pass before you discover your mishap. Immediately, you phone the coffee shop, but you're told that no one turned it in. Panic strikes as you assess what you've lost and what you need to do to avoid a greater loss. The pain of dealing with this aggravates you.

First, you'll have to cancel all your credit cards, and that means spending a few hours on hold calling credit card companies. Then you'll have to run to the department of motor vehicles and apply for a replacement driver's license. That's always fun. Oh, and you can kiss that $52 in cash goodbye along with those cute photos of your dog wearing a sailor's hat and the last photo you had of you and your son at his sixth-grade dance. Then you'll need a new library card, a video rental card, and a bunch of frequent shopper and diners discount cards.

Although the loss gives you a major migraine, you mostly feel pained by the disruption in your routine and the plans you had that day. None of these tasks in and of itself is overwhelming—and you won't face financial ruin because of your loss—but collectively having to reassemble the contents that go into the new wallet (oh yeah, that's something else you'll need to replace) throws you off stride. You certainly don't need this mental and emotional disruption.

Mental and Emotional Disruption

Employee turnover represents a similar mental and emotional disruption for managers who have myriad tasks to do. The sick feeling you get in your stomach when I detail losing your purse or wallet mirrors the one you get when one of your Opies turns in their resignation. It's not the end of the world, and it certainly won't put you out of business. But what a gigantic interruption in your plans! Suddenly, everything changes because you have to search for a replacement.

Every time you lose a kidployee (particularly one who is a Solid Subordinate or higher on the GAD continuum), you think, "Damn, didn't I just go through all of this?" Maybe you feel like the character Bill Murray played in the movie *Groundhog Day;* no matter how hard you brace yourself, every time you turn around, it's February 2 and you've got to relive the same brain damage. You have no assurance that tomorrow won't be Groundhog Day all over again.

Just Get Another Warm Body, Right?

Don't be fooled into believing that when a kidployee quits, the costs of replacement are minimal if you can quickly hire someone else to do the job. After all, we're only talking about a low-wage, front-line employee. Isn't perpetual staffing on the front line just part of your job?

Still, recruiting, hiring, and training a replacement is never a snap, regardless of how prepared you are. It not only taxes your time and energy, it also places an added burden on coworkers who have to adjust their schedules and pick up the slack. If some are already on the brink of quitting, the additional workload might send them over the edge. Previously committed kidployees feeling close ties to the departing Opie could suddenly find themselves less attached to their jobs and split, too.

When you hire a new recruit (or when one is hired for you), you hope this newbie at least possesses some job skills and can hit the ground running with little direction. More times than not, however, it doesn't work that way. The new staffer doesn't have the right practical, real-world experience. While appearing streetwise, they could be totally lost in a work environment. Plus, you don't have any time to give them a crash course in work ethic, and you have only limited time to teach them basic skills. As a result, your

> Make no mistake about it; one good kid leaving your business can spark a whole bevy of kidployees to break away.

customers, who were accustomed to receiving great service by your departing Opie, will have to adapt to less-than-acceptable service while
your newbie slowly adjusts.

Incorrect New Hires

There's another consideration. After you've committed the time
and made the effort to hire and train a replacement, what if you discover
you've brought in the wrong person for the job? Perhaps your new kidployee looked good on paper and interviewed well but simply doesn't
have what it takes. Maybe that kid doesn't fit in with the chemistry of
your team or take direction well. The kid might prove undependable or,
worse, untrustworthy.

Many managers with the responsibility of hiring tend to lose sight of
the seemingly obvious notion that high turnover largely results from bad
hiring to begin with. If you have the wrong person in the wrong position,
you're spending time, energy, and effort on someone who predictably
will leave the company within months or even weeks—causing all kinds
of grief during the interim.

Bringing in the wrong people only compounds the costs and the disruption factor. If you make a bad hiring decision, you have to figure out
how to move your newbies into a slot where they can be productive or
face terminating them quickly. Unfortunately, a termination could further exacerbate an already delicate situation among the other members
of your staff.

WHAT ARE YOUR KIDPLOYEES THINKING?

According to a 2004 Gallup survey, at any given moment, 62 percent
of an organization's work force is actively seeking a new job and would
be ready to leave if a better opportunity emerges.

The High Costs of Low Retention

Industry studies show that employee turnover depressed earnings
and stock prices of American businesses by an average of 38 cents per
share across the board. This frightening number is totally unacceptable
to upper management and proves that retaining kidployees should

demand your close attention, regardless of the kind or the size of business you operate.

The costs associated with hiring and training a new employee far exceed what some managers might think. Aside from experiencing a dip in productivity and potentially losing sales, getting a new person up to speed could result in higher overtime costs, because existing kidployees have to work more hours to fill in the gaps. Naturally, hiring new young employees means bracing for costly rookie errors, the likelihood of accidents, and the expense of uniforms and equipment. And, if you're replacing a kidployee you had to fire, you might also face an unemployment claim that increases your unemployment tax.

And don't forget the ultimate nightmare scenario. What if the kidployee you recruited, trained, and built a close relationship with not only resigns but leaves your employ to work for your biggest competitor? Now you've aided and abetted the enemy. This is akin to running to your bank, making a large withdrawal, then sprinting to your competitor's bank and depositing those funds. Double whammy!

The Intangibles

Suppose I come to your café each morning for a bagel and a cup of coffee. Within a few weeks, Jessie, your morning help, recognizes me every time I come to the counter. We kid around a little, and she even memorizes my standard order. After one month, when Jessie sees my car pull up outside, she immediately pours a tall, double latte and pops a multigrain bagel in the toaster, knowing in advance what I'll order. "Good morning, Mr. C!" she greets me as I walk in. "I saved your favorite table for you by the window, and I'll get your breakfast right out to you with the morning paper."

At that point, the bagel and coffee become props in a bigger scenario, because a whole new level of service is taking place. With this kind of attention, your café transforms into my own version of the bar in *Cheers!* I can't even think about starting my day any other way. Jessie represents Sam; I represent Norm.

Then one morning, I come in to find Jessie gone. I ask where she is, and the new person, Kyle, tells me she's no longer with the company. It saddens me, but heck, it's just a kid at a bagel place. However, now I must explain to Kyle how to make my latte exactly the way Jessie did. I have to tell him how to toast my bagel and put just a dab of light cream cheese on it the way Jessie did. And then I tell him he needs to start looking for me each morning because, well, I'm a regular you know, and I deserve what I'm used to getting.

You see, a guy can stop for coffee and a bagel at a whole lot of places between my house and your café. I went out of my way because Jessie made my day. I really don't want to have to "train" Kyle, but I will. However, if Kyle doesn't catch on in a hurry, you can bet I'll find another place to hang out in the morning.

Ask any bank manager how the turnover on the front line can kill you. Most of us want to walk into our "home" bank and be acknowledged, then transact business with a familiar face. We certainly don't appreciate being asked for our identification (even if we have Bill Gates as a co-signer) every time we want to withdraw a roll of nickels.

Unfortunately, the tellers at most banks revolve faster than the front doors and every time we walk to the counter, a brand new kidployee stands between us and our money. It doesn't seem to matter if we've been at that bank since dinosaurs roamed the earth; we're treated as if we're trying to cash a two-party, out-of-state counter check on a closed account: definitely not a way to build long-term customer relations.

WHAT INDUSTRY IS IMMUNE?

In almost any industry, employee turnover becomes a time-consuming, energy-draining challenge, if not an outright ordeal, that you'd avoid if you could. In the fast-food industry, for example, annual turnover often exceeds 300 percent. The overall cost of employee turnover as a percentage of total fast-food industry earnings is 16 percent. As costly as this is, the number rises in industries with higher wages.

Specifically, in specialty retailing, annual turnover can range as high as 97 percent, nearly matching that of the fast-food industry. The cost of this turnover as a percentage of industry earnings can equal 50 percent. Again, this is primarily due to the higher salaries among specialty retailing staff and a wide array of other costs associated with losing and regaining competent help. Besides the monetary cost of turnover, a more dangerous result is losing the knowledge the young people take with them.

Testing to Reduce Turnover Costs

A growing number of companies recognize the value of giving employment candidates tests and/or assessments to reduce their turnover rates. Although such tests are far from perfect, they have a high degree of effectiveness in many situations.

By administering a test that can rate the personality and motivation of job candidates, recruiters can better select those who best match the existing company culture.

Tom Decotiis, managing partner of Decotiis Erhard, a consulting firm based in Colorado Springs, Colorado, observes that by evaluating the personalities of job candidates along with their job-related skills, recruiters' chances of making successful hires improve markedly. According to one study, the funds spent on recruiting, hiring, orientation, training, turnover, and lost productivity equal 150 percent of an employee's annual salary.

Decotiis says, "A major cause of job dissatisfaction and the desire to quit is the quality of the people you work with." So if a kidployee comes to be part of a team and is the wrong person for the job, they can affect the morale of all the other team members. If their performances suffer as a result, costs shoot up even more.

Judging Character Is Tricky

Unfortunately, many managers are not good judges of character, especially when meeting with a job candidate for a brief time and trying to "fill in the blanks" on the fly. This approach rarely works. Robert Fox, executive vice president of marketing at MindData Systems in Dallas, says, "You'll always find someone with the right credentials, but if they don't have the right attitude, they aren't going to work out." MindData Systems offers Web-based evaluation tools that help managers overcome their built-in biases.

Interviewing can be a highly inexact process, especially when screening young people, who can often figure out which answer they need to give to land the job instead of responding with how they really think or feel. They get to know what to say and know how to act to impress the interviewer. They realize it doesn't take a budding Einstein to put one over on an interviewer, especially if the interviewer has had a long, busy workday and is juggling different responsibilities just to make it through to the end.

Sometimes harried managers who need additional staff immediately project onto the job candidate what they'd like to see. Only later do they realize they brought in someone who's unlike the person they presumed they hired during their brief, inexact, fragmented, and inconclusive interview.

A SOCIALLY PERVASIVE PROBLEM

Whether you're a business owner, a manager, or a consumer, you are affected by turnover among kidployees. After all, excellence can only be developed over time, so if kidployees aren't investing themselves over any extended period, they don't fully develop. If this trend continues, excellence as a measure of quality, productivity, and service will evaporate.

You've marinated in misery long enough. It's time to discover how to get your kidployees to stick around long enough to train them to be outstanding assets to your company. So step out of the swamp, wipe off the muck, and read the balance of this section for ideas and solutions that, when put in place, will transform your kidployees' ability to make solid contributions for the long haul.

9

COMPENSATION:
SHARE THE LOVE

Standing in the middle of the crowded concourse B at Denver International Airport, I scanned the eateries on both sides of me looking for a place to grab a sandwich and drink to take on board a two-hour flight. Anticipating hunger pangs and hearing the final boarding announcement, I knew I only had a few minutes. I certainly wasn't going to be picky; I just needed something edible, and I needed it quick. But the lines at the fast food restaurants surrounding me were so crowded that I realized if I waited in any of them, I'd certainly miss my flight.

I gave up on the idea of lunch. Instead, I pulled out my digital camera to take candid photos of the kidployees working in each of these nationally franchised restaurants. You see, it puzzled me that even though business was extremely strong, the employees were moving at a moderate pace as if their customers had plenty of time. Surely many other travelers like me would have spent money at these restaurants if the lines were moving faster.

My camera couldn't record the relaxed pace these kidployees were moving at, but it did capture the looks of boredom and even despair on their faces. "How come these kidployees aren't happy?" I wondered. "With the cash registers ringing up tons of sales, they should be making their respective owner/managers extremely happy."

Then it hit me.

Yes, the owner/managers are happy to see lots of people waiting to spend money at their restaurants, because they'll make more money, but the kidployees make the same amount at busy times as when there are no customers. Besides, when activity is low, they can blast their music, talk to each other, and maybe even call a friend from their cell phones. I quickly realized I was witnessing a classic win-lose situation: when the restaurant owner/managers were winning, the kidployees were losing. They have absolutely zero incentive to work harder, faster, or better—or even provide the slightest hint of customer service. In this counterintuitive environment, no wonder these employees weren't smiling or working efficiently.

Start Thinking Digital

You and I have been completely brainwashed to believe in the wage-per-hour form of employee compensation. That's how we were paid when we came into the workplace, so that seems to be the only way to pay our employees now. But as long as we remain stuck in the wage-time dichotomy, we're imposing an obsolete, analog method of compensation onto digital-thinking employees. This is a train wreck just waiting to happen.

The solution? If you want them to give a damn about your business or your customers, make certain you give them some vested interest in the profitability of your business. Find ways to reward them when business jumps and efficiency reigns. Otherwise, they'll expend zero mental or physical energy to try to increase revenues; they'll even refuse to go out of their way to reduce waste or inventory shrinkage.

Who has the biggest impact on each of these factors? Your front-line kidployees. Therefore, doesn't it make sense to compensate them for their role in each of these factors?

Minimum Daily Requirement

Although they might not say it, here's what your hourly kidployees often think: "I can make your business grow, but if I don't see any immediate return for my time and talents in doing so, then all you're going to get from me is the Minimum Daily Requirement (MDR)."

Analog thinking says, "Pay me for my time."

Digital thinking says, "Pay me for my time when just being there is the only thing you require of me. But if you want me to invest myself while I am at the job, pay me for my talents. Just tell me what needs to be done, then let me figure out how to do it. I'm technosavvy, and I can produce amazingly well if I know it will work to my advantage as well as yours."

Results Trump Time

Wage-per-hour compensation can be an effective place to start, but don't think it's the alpha and omega just because it's the easiest method to calculate wages.

If your business requires manufacturing, you probably establish production quotas for your front line. Your calculations might show that a minimum of ten units an hour per employee is needed to turn a profit. But if your kidployees can consistently produce more than ten, they should be compensated accordingly. If, on the other hand, your kidployees can produce 10 units in 45 minutes and higher compensation doesn't motivate them to produce more, then for heaven sakes, let them work shorter shifts and leave earlier. If they determine they can put in the MDR and meet your ten-unit-per-hour standard, you'll never tap into their incredible abilities and will, in essence, disenfranchise them. Your compensation plan could turn a talented kidployee into a mediocre, disengaged, robotic front-liner who never exceeds ten units per hour—a tragic waste of their time and your money.

Compensation and Longevity

You face an inherent danger if you base kidployees' compensation solely on length of service. Plus, if the only bonus system you offer is one in which each staff member automatically receives $.50 an hour each month or so, you're sending a resounding message that "not quitting" is more important than high performance. In effect, you're telling your front-liners that success in your company means doing just enough to avoid being fired.

Certainly, spending time on the job is a prerequisite to excellence; no employees can be at their most productive state providing their highest value on day one. However, just showing up itself doesn't guarantee excellence, much less performance. Perhaps their aim is to coast without much effort.

Teachers might be at their best after only three years of experience, but if their compensation ties directly to how long they teach in that district, then excellence means nothing. If the only goal is meeting tenure,

union-scale wage compensation systems become huge deterrents to performance, productivity, and excellence. The best and the
brightest young teachers soon realize that
making an extra effort to be outstanding
isn't worth a nickel. And even though bright
young teachers might be twice as effective as
the burned out ones in the next classroom,
those with tenure make more than double
the salary. It's not fair. No wonder schools are
in trouble.

> Kidployees want to be acknowledged when they put forth difficult, quality work. If they go to the wall for you, compensate them for it—or at the very least acknowledge them and share the glory.

However, although your kidployee compensation plan should be tied
to performance, it shouldn't overlook loyalty and length of service. Longevity leads to competence; competence is a precursor to contribution.

To create an effective compensation plan, combine length of service
with performance. If a kidployee does progressively better work and stays
on for a longer time, this helps your business grow, so make sure they take
part in that growth.

Don't Tie Compensation to Position

Here's what happens every day in sales. Some hotshot sales rep rakes
in the sales, setting company records on the fly. Upper management notices and thinks, "Hmmm. Let's promote this person into sales management and have other reps report to them." The record-setting sales rep
then becomes a manager and no longer calls on clients and closes deals.
They now work with low-achieving reps and take care of paperwork and
reports. In no time, their once-stellar reputation with upper management becomes tarnished, they begin to hate the job, and then they leave
the company. This person simply wasn't cut out for management.

If the only way to boost the compensation of your front-liners is to
promote them to higher-paid positions away from the front line, then
your system sabotages your organization's own growth. In effect, you are
an internal corporate raider. Taking fantastic front-line kidployees and
teaching them to supervise others removes them from what they probably do best and love the most.

You don't want to pigeonhole any of your kidployees into remaining
in one particular position, so find a way to compensate them for the
good job they're doing in their current position. That way, if they want
to move upward, the motivation won't be just to make more money. Use

your power of promotion only when it serves the interests of everyone involved, not just as the only way to justify more compensation.

Creative Compensation

Suppose, however, you're employing front-line staffers who work the cash register. They earn $7.25 an hour whether or not there's a huge line in front of them. How could you reward kidployees appropriately for those hours in which they face a never-ending sea of customers versus those when business slows down so much, you barely need anybody on board?

Perhaps you could offer them a 10 percent increase in salary for any one-hour period in which they key more than $200 in sales. Or you could base added compensation on how many customers a kidployee handles. Or follow the Eddie Bauer model that rewards all employees based on overall store performance, which promotes more bonding and a teamlike atmosphere.

Less of What You Don't Want

You could even arrange extra compensation based on the number of complaints or, in this case, the lack thereof. For example, any employee on a four-hour shift who receives two complaints or fewer would be rewarded accordingly. You could even devise a plan based on a simple formula—not rocket science—that kidployees can follow. Here's an example:

A 10 percent hourly increase is based on the number of customers one encounters, the number of cash register ring-ups, and the overall sales volume, minus the number of complaints or mishaps. You'd weigh the factors proportionately and, in that way, give everyone an opportunity for increased compensation.

Go Platinum!

Experiment with creative ways to reward employees based on their individual goals and objectives. Don't assume they want more money just because that motivates you. Today, the Golden Rule has been replaced by the Platinum Rule, "Do unto others as they would have you do unto

The inherent danger of bestowing rewards only for results is that you might only receive big results. Consequently, you could be training your people to go for the big sale while ignoring small ones. You could be encouraging them to maximize the short term while shortchanging the long term. Plus, rewarding for results might disproportionately favor those who actually write up the sale while ignoring those back-liners who contribute in supporting positions.

them." In other words, reward their efforts and the results they create in the way that fits their tastes, needs, and sense of style.

The once-popular one-size-fits-all compensation plan is on its way out. What motivates one member of your team might be a disincentive for another. Naturally, if you want to reward kidployees based on individual preferences, you need to determine what those preferences are. That requires getting to know them individually and asking a lot of questions. Although this research might take time and effort on your part, it will greatly diminish the enormous amount of time, energy, and money you spend on the hire-fire-hire-fire treadmill.

A LITTLE INCENTIVE GOES A LONG WAY

Bonuses don't have to be in the form of cash. In many cases, they work better when they're not. The server in a restaurant who relies heavily on tips will encounter times when restaurant activity slows down for one reason or another. Managers who want to score points with a worker in this circumstance might reach into their desk drawers and pull out movie tickets or gift certificates to a favorite store.

C a s e   S t u d y

COMPENSATION AT EDDIE BAUER

Kidployees of Eddie Bauer stores remain in their positions longer than those at competing retailers because of the company's unique compensation plan. In its 400-plus stores in the United States, Eddie Bauer employs 62,000 front-line employees, approximately 85 percent of its total workforce. They perform typical retail functions including sales, cash register operations, stocking, and so on.

To recruit top young talent and subsequently motivate and retain them, Eddie Bauer offers wage incentives amounting to an additional 6.5 percent of base pay when store goals are met. For example, a worker earning minimum wage could look forward to an extra $18.61 a week or $74.44 a month, when the store achieves an established sales goal. In 2003, 95 percent of the stores reached their monthly sales goal at least once during the year. Through the first half of 2004, 84 percent of all stores met or exceeded their monthly sales targets.

Sales goals differ from store to store depending on their sales history, location, and customer traffic. When a store reaches its goal, hourly employees receive an additional 35 cents an hour. If the store exceeds that goal by a large margin, they can receive up to an additional 65 cents an hour. Eddie Bauer systematically tracks the time and attendance of its workers. Bonuses are calculated based on this data, which eliminates the chance of employee favoritism or human error.

This "team store initiative" type of compensation plan clearly entices store employees to work as a team. Managers like the program and acknowledge that it gives kidployees a stake in the store's success.

Case Study

A NICE SURPRISE AT ENTERPRISE

As a frequent traveler, I'd achieved top-level customer status with Hertz, Avis, and National car rental companies, but I had never rented from Enterprise. I had always heard they were slightly different than the others—but I didn't know how. With the other car rental companies, speed is their primary concern. An agent quickly issues you a rental form, gives you keys, points you to a car, and sends you on your way. When you come back, a return agent meets you at your car, scans your mileage and fuel level, and prints out a receipt on the spot.

When I arrived at the Enterprise counter, I noticed their agents were all in their early 20s. Although they didn't wear uniforms, they were dressed professionally in white shirts, ties, and dress slacks/skirts. These agents were much friendlier, more knowledgeable, and much more eager to please me than those at the other three companies I'd worked with—and I had no status whatsoever with Enterprise. After we finished the paperwork at the front desk, the rental agent walked out to the car with me as we continued our pleasant conversation. Then he inspected the car with me to make certain it was what I wanted and, now knowing the purpose of my visit, suggested upgrades that would make my stay more comfortable and efficient.

Employees of the other companies routinely ask, "Do you want the insurance option?" which I simply decline. This kid explained that after a long flight in an unfamiliar city, the probability of my having a mishap would be much greater than I might imagine. "But with your authorization, I can make certain that you have all the peace of mind you'll need." He went on to say, "You'll be traveling a long distance on this trip, and being a big guy (a compliment to me), you'd be more comfortable in a slightly larger car." He walked me to a Buick and said, "This model has a climate control system to keep you cool, and it has a much smoother ride." I knew he was attempting to up-sell me, but his approach was different, refreshing, and welcome. I had the distinct feeling that he was focused on my best interests. Paying a little more actually translated into a better value for me.

Completely impressed with his demeanor, professionalism, and vested interests in my safety and comfort, I bought every upgrade and coverage he suggested—and left feeling good about it.

As I got in the car to leave, I just had to ask him, "You could obviously work in a more glamorous or high-paying position. Why do you work for Enterprise?"

His answer intrigued me. "Enterprise came to my college campus looking for management trainees. I was graduating with a degree in liberal arts and had no idea what I was going to do with my degree. The recruiter told me I had the makings of a future star with this incredible company. He offered me an opportunity to grow with Enterprise and to move quickly into a partnership-type capacity. To do so meant I'd have to learn every aspect of the business, from the front counter to renting the cars to cleaning them and bringing them back in. I was told I'd have to put in long hours and I'd only earn a modest first-year salary. If I demonstrated I could handle it, I'd have my own store—and an unlimited income—in a few short years."

He went on to tell me about Enterprise's car sales division. In addition to my needing to rent a car on this occasion, did I also want to buy a car? Used cars from rent-a-car companies are actually a decent value,

Enterprise management says to its young recruits, "When our customers are delighted, we are successful. And our success will be your success."

because the cars are fully inspected each time they're returned by customers, plus they're sold after one year at competitive prices with a comprehensive warranty. Understandably, this trainee would earn a significant sum if he provided the company with referrals to these sales.

I said to him, "You're probably making less than some of your friends who recently graduated." He said, "Yes, I am, and they rib me about it all the time. But they're thinking about today, and I'm thinking about three to five years down the line. I know almost with certainly that I'm going to catch them and pass them. People in this company who joined right out of college have retired after 25 years with an incredible salary and a long-term retirement package. And these are division managers, not corporate bigwigs at headquarters. I know I can make it to the top."

He then excitedly told me that he was among the top 10 percent of the new Enterprise trainees in terms of revenue generated and customer satisfaction. If he stays in the upper 10 percent, within six months, he'll receive a huge bonus on top of everything he already mentioned. In a few years, he would move into management where his salary would more than double. Within a decade, his salary could be ten times his current base salary.

As he opened up more, he told me he earns a significant bonus when he receives a customer's company business. That's when a customer comes in and rents a car, likes the service, and decides to use Enterprise for all of their company's business. When the customer signs on and receives volume discounts, free upgrades, and other perks, the rep gets some of that revenue.

I realized this young man was speaking volumes about the way Enterprise values its kidployees. The company provides a clear career path so managers can measure employee progress at every point along the trail. Front-line employees have a vested interest in customer sales and satisfaction. Because of the way Enterprise has structured its career path and relationships with young trainees, buy-in is high and business is booming.

WHAT CAN YOU DO DIFFERENTLY?

Evaluate your own compensation plan by answering these questions:

- Does your company provide an "enterprising" career track that encourages young talent to give a damn about image, profits, and long-term company success?
- From your kidployees' perspective, does *your* success equate to *their* success, or do they think they have to work harder just to line your pockets?
- Are additional profit incentives built into your employees' compensation plan? If so, are they clearly laid out?
- Are these incentives challenging but reachable? (Think Eddie Bauer.)
- Are you conveying to your kidployees that it's to everyone's advantage to turn a one-time customer into a long-time customer? (Think Enterprise.)

10

RECOGNITION: DOES ANYONE NOTICE?

She loved her job as a barista. At 16, my daughter Whitney felt she had found her calling. She wore the green apron with pride and enjoyed making and serving the vast array of coffee drinks famous the world over.

The store where she worked was situated inside a large chain bookstore in a long strip shopping plaza next to a 12-screen movie theater. Whitney had no objections working weekend evenings because all the "cool kids" came in after their movies for a cup of java. She preferred the chaotic traffic over the much slower, "boring" afternoon hours. Besides, she earned more in tips and the time flew by.

One Friday evening, she came home about an hour-and-a-half late. Exhausted, she didn't want to talk about work and went straight to bed. When she woke up on Saturday morning, she described how two of the four kids scheduled to work on Friday had called in sick, leaving her and one other employee to handle the entire workload. "We were swamped all night long, Dad. I didn't have two minutes to eat anything, take a break, or even to use the bathroom. After the last customer left, Marissa and I spent two hours cleaning up the place and balancing out the register."

I empathized with her but felt confident that her boss would soon be calling to praise her for her efforts. An hour later, Mr. Wilson called, but not to thank and praise Whitney. Instead, he asked her why she and Marissa hadn't cleaned the inside of the glass in the brownie case. His call upset Whitney and left me aghast. I'd seen this as a golden opportunity for Mr. Wilson to ratchet Whitney's GAD score up two or three points. After all, he had made out like a bandit because Friday's sales were extremely high and his payroll costs for the evening were cut in half. Although his two kidployees were clearly outmanned and understaffed, they had held down the fort and left the store in respectable shape. But instead of calling to thank and praise her—even offer her a paid night off or a $20 bonus—Mr. Wilson focused all his attention on the one thing the girls didn't do completely. Within two weeks, both Whitney and Marissa resigned and the coffee shop manager was left with the arduous and costly task of having to replace these two Opies.

Positive Reinforcement

When it comes to managing your kidployees, the age-old axiom "behavior that gets rewarded gets repeated" takes on renewed meaning. Some of your younger employees have grown up with doting parents and expect praise for even the slightest achievement. Others, who never received the recognition they deserved, desperately look for anyone to take notice when they perform admirably.

So which of these two types of kidployee require positive reinforcement? They both do. And the optimal word here is *require*.

Every successful employer of 16- to 24-year-old front-liners develops a handbook that clearly articulates company policies and procedures. Executives go to great expense to prepare managers with the tools to handle common employee problems, so they're not caught off guard when a kid doesn't show up for work, reports in wearing an unkempt uniform, acts snooty with a customer, and so on. Sadly, most of these handbooks offer few tools to prepare managers to recognize and reward the kidployees who excel in the workplace. These managers don't know how to reaffirm the kid who wipes down the front door without being told to do so, the one who consistently shows up on time in a freshly laundered uniform, or the employee who helps a new coworker learn a tricky procedure.

Doesn't it stand to reason that if what is rewarded is repeated, then what is ignored is not repeated? Pretty soon, the kid who puts in the extra effort but gets no reward (or even

> You can't get your kidployees to buy in to your way of doing things unless you reward them as they move up on the GAD continuum. Simply stated, the moment you stop noticing is the moment they stop improving.

a simple acknowledgment) begins to ask, "Why bother?" If he continues to feel slighted, a potential Opie can eventually grow horns and end up hanging a *Closed* sign on your door, as I did at the Pagoda restaurant.

What a Wise Manager Does

Wise managers keep their eyes open for new and creative ways to reward those kidployees who do report on time, dress appropriately, provide excellent service, and so on. These managers continually look for opportunities to recognize effort and performance. Not wanting to forget anyone, they actually keep a written record of how many times each kidployee is acknowledged and encouraged. Ken Blanchard, noted management guru and author of the perennial bestseller *The One-Minute Manager*, summed it best up when he said, "Catch them doing something right."

It's important to note that we're no longer talking about employee compensation and benefits. Those are negotiated terms that are mutually agreed upon, expected at regular intervals, and legally enforced. Look at your compensation package as the main course and your recognition and rewards program as the dessert. You can adequately feed dinner guests with meat and potatoes, but if you want them to come back, appeal to their sweet tooth.

FOUR Ps OF WISE RECOGNITION AND REWARDS

There are numerous ways to give a kid a pat on the back. The best formula for recognizing and rewarding positive performances of your kidployees follow these four criteria:

1. *Personal.* Whitney loves music and is always talking about the latest and hottest CDs. Anyone who took an active interest could determine this fact in five minutes. If Mr. Wilson had wanted to give Whitney a perk for her effort on Friday night, one idea would have been to add a $20 bonus to her weekly check. A far better alternative would have been to hand her a gift certificate for a free CD at her favorite music store. This would have cost 25 percent less than the monetary bonus, but it would have meant a thousand times more to Whitney. Here's the key point: regardless of the type of recognition and reward given, its perceived value

escalates when it's individualized for the employee. Although tailor-making rewards requires more time and consideration, the resulting benefits certainly justify the extra thought and energy. Yes, this does mean that you've got to know your kidployees on a different level, discovering what they like to do in their personal time. But this extra effort enables you to show a kidployee that you value them enough to do something special for them.

2. *Proportionate.* Just as it proved costly for Mr. Wilson to overlook his kidployees' added contributions, it would have been just as foolish to have given them each a $100 bonus. Overzealous managers, who are quick to heap praise and incentives on employees for minor things, find it hard to keep showing a proportionate amount of enthusiasm for bigger accomplishments. To keep them moving up the GAD continuum, any recognition or reward should always match the level of performance being recognized.

   Realize that, by giving too much of a reward for a small accomplishment, you could paint yourself into a corner. That's why preplanning your recognition and reward program is imperative so you know what to do at various levels of achievement.

3. *Prompt.* Young people live in the moment. Rewarding them with a dollar today is far more effective than giving them two dollars tomorrow. Wise managers know this and are always prepared to reward positive behavior promptly. If you can easily lay your hands on the form your company uses to write up an employee who does wrong, then you should have something equally as handy to reward the employee who goes above and beyond.

   In that vein, don't tell them that you'll pay for their dinner out; hand them a certificate at a designated restaurant and give them a night off. When giving a cash award, don't tell them you'll add $20 to their next paycheck; reach into your pocket and hand them a $20 bill. Immediacy doubles the impact of any reward.

4. *Public.* The value of the reward you present will multiply exponentially if it's given to a kid while friends and peers look on. The recipient wants to know they are doing well, but they also want to let their friends and coworkers in on the secret.

   Imagine both the short-term and long-term impression if you ran out to the front counter, rang a bell to get the attention of your customers, and said, "Ladies and gentlemen, Ian has worked here for six months, and he has never missed a day! We can always count on Ian, and he's a big reason we can give the ultimate in customer service. Ian loves auto racing, so we're sending Ian and his guest out to the track to see the drag championships this weekend. Please raise the roof for Ian!"

When a situation prohibits praising or rewarding a kid in public, consider sharing the news on the company Web site or message board or even posting a congratulatory announcement in a highly visible place. When Mr. Wilson phoned on Saturday, it would have been impossible to praise Whitney in the company of her peers. He could have, however, told the other employees about the events of Friday evening during the next employee meeting. This not only would have made Whitney and Marissa feel special, it would have let the other employees know that excellence doesn't go unnoticed or unrewarded.

What to Recognize

The sign above the patient's chair in my dentist's office reads, "You don't have to floss all your teeth. Only the ones you want to keep." That wisdom also applies when it comes to your recognition and reward program. It's simply not enough to acknowledge your kidployees' efforts in sales and customer service. If you want to encourage excellence in all phases of your business, include rewarding achievement in those phases or they will decay.

The owner of a large hardware store in Chicago employs 25 high school and college students. He and his managers created a program to present *You WOWed 'em!* cards to kidployees whom they saw giving great service to customers. The kids were told that when they collected five cards, they could turn them in for a $25 cash award. At first, the program was met with great excitement and it seemed to nudge the entire front line a few points upward on the GAD scale. But soon after, he noticed that his program was taking a negative toll on other areas of his operation.

The hardware store kidployees suddenly became so eager to help customers that they neglected jobs like stocking, sweeping, and general maintenance. After punching in, his front-liners just milled around the store looking for someone they could WOW. Although

When he was president and CEO of General Electric, Jack Welch sent a letter to shareholders stating, "The top 20 percent of our employees should be loved, nurtured, and rewarded in the soul and the wallet, because they are the ones that make our magic happen. Losing one of these people must be held up as a leadership sin—a real failing."

customers did notice a huge increase in service, the store's appearance declined sharply. So the managers stopped the WOW program. Soon, though, the store looked much better, but customer service fell off.

A few weeks later, management reintroduced the WOW program, only this time, kidployees could also earn WOW cards for demonstrating excellence in seven additional areas that didn't involve customer interaction. With the new program, service improved dramatically, and so did the appearance of the store, product merchandising, attendance and punctuality, safety efforts, and so on.

Outstanding performance comes in all shapes and sizes. You don't need to reward excellence in all phases of your business, only in those areas requiring excellence. Make certain that your recognition and rewards program reaches deep into all phases of your operation, and you'll see improvements across the board.

The Cost of Recognition

Don't be fooled into believing that to recognize and reward achievement, you constantly have to reach into your wallet. While it helps to allocate some resources to reward demonstrated excellence, many of the best methods won't cost you a dime.

For example, consider calling the parents of an outstanding kidployee just to tell them how terrifically their son or daughter is doing. You could also make contact with them via e-mail. Hand a kid a note saying, "Good job," or offer to wash their car as a way of saying, "You've gone out of your way for me, so let me go out of my way for you." You can recognize achievement in countless ways without spending money. With thoughtfulness and a touch of creativity, you can assure a continuation in the positive attitude, behaviors, and performance of your front line.

Pitfalls and Traps

Opponents of recognition and reward programs believe it's easy to condition others to a level of expectation where, like a trained seal, they might stop doing tricks if they don't always receive a special treat. Although the concept is controversial, it does bring up a valid point.

Your kidployees need and want to be recognized, but if you institute a program that goes overboard, you could end up in trouble. The WOW card program created by the hardware store backfired at first, and management had to react fast to correct the difficulties and right the ship.

Ultimately, businesses that routinely select an Employee of the Month often motivate one employee and demotivate many others. Kidployees who believe they should have received an award but didn't might rebel. Some kidployees think the idea of having their name on a plaque in the front of the store is lame, so they go to great lengths not to win. But the truth is, unless it comes bundled with a premium parking space and some other cool perks, the Employee of the Month idea fails to resonate with today's young talent.

I've seen employee contests blow up and destroy the team environment of many businesses. This happens when management announces a competition among employees based on who sells the most, has the fewest customer complaints, or works the most hours. Sometimes these contests bring about the desired result, but often they lead to catastrophe, with kidployees fighting for customers or territory, sabotaging each other's efforts, or falling far enough behind that they completely give up.

If you want to create across-the-board results and increase the GAD factor of all your employees while maintaining the spirit of teamwork and camaraderie, have the participants compete against a standard—not each other. Examples in this scenario would include: any employee who can sell more than 50 units by next Tuesday receives an iPod, or we'll take the entire department to dinner and a movie if no one misses a scheduled day during the Christmas season.

C *ase* **S** *tudy*

SPIKING SERVICE AT SUMNER

In 2002, senior staff members of Sumner Regional Health Systems (SRHS), which employs more than 1,500 associates, caught wind of a patient satisfaction initiative that was sweeping attitudes out of the gutter and onto the road to success.

While SRHS had no visible signs of low morale and its financial state was good—in fact, above average—the senior staff had long been committed to becoming a stand-out organization. Its members also realized that organizations don't have to experience a crisis before initiating a plan to go from good to great.

The excellence initiative they witnessed was led by Quint Studer of The Studer Group, an organization dedicated to making hospitals great places to work and great places to receive care. The Group's program, designed for the health care industry but applying universal fundamentals, is based on this idea: to raise patient satisfaction (thus increasing business for the hospital), hospitals must first make their associates happy.

Quint Studer's argument was convincing. If your front-line workers aren't happy, how can you expect them to give their customers (in this case, their patients) the best possible service? After all, it's tough for nurses who feel disgruntled to say, "We're going to take very good care of you today," and it's even tougher for patients to believe they actually mean it.

Little things often go unnoticed in a hospital in the wake of giving good care and saving lives. But many nurses do things that aren't in their job titles—like sitting on the edge of the bed crying with a woman who's just lost her baby or making a special run to a drive-through to buy a chocolate milkshake for a sick child.

SRHS leaders decided to recognize actions like these by creating a program called "Spikes"—implying that employees use railroad spikes to keep the SRHS Excellence Express train moving forward on its journey from good to great. Anyone who does something above and beyond adds a spike to the train track and gets the organization closer to its goal of delivering great care.

More than 100 managers and directors are assigned to distribute Spikes, which are awarded within 24 hours of an associate's extraordinary act. Once employees have collected five Spikes, they turn them in for a miniature Gold Spike that they wear on their name badges. They also earn a trip to the "tinderbox" where they can pull out goodies like a $15 gift certificate to their favorite restaurant, a free car wash, or a pair of movie tickets. Some associates have collected as many as 50 Spikes, which means they've visited the tinderbox 10 times in the past few years.

When SRHS first rolled out the program, Spikes were awarded for prompt service, showing up to work on time so the next shift could start promptly, delivering the answer to a question the same day instead of the following day, or picking up trash in the hallway. As the program progressed and a culture of rewards and recognition became established, the expectations of Spike-worthy behavior have increased. For example, associates now get rewarded for completing a huge project ahead of schedule, for making sure the man in room 206 receives extra sugar every time he gets his coffee, for taking time to explain a complex medical procedure to a patient's troubled spouse, or for voluntarily helping a coworker finish something at the last minute.

Many managers make an announcement to the entire staff when giving a Spike to an associate, so others can see what types of behavior are rewarded. Trips to the tinderbox are also public. A member of the rewards and recognition committee brings the box to the lunch area every other week for two hours. During that time, all associates who have five Spikes or more can come by and turn them in for a gift. The Spike itself is simply a slip of paper with an image of a railroad spike and a place to write the recipient's name and their special job performance. All Spikes get reviewed later to help management determine who will be named Associates of the Month.

Since starting the program in 2002, SRHS has conducted two employee satisfaction surveys to assess morale in their three different hospitals. In 2000, employee satisfaction levels hovered around the 74th percentile, which indicates low employee morale when compared with other organizations (a C–). Two-and-a-half years later—after implementing Sumner's Golden Spike program—the survey placed SRHS in the 99th percentile (an A+) and showed that 79 percent of the associates had positive morale. In this mentally draining business, the national average for positive morale in health care organizations is between 40 to 60 percent. Sumner now ranks number one in employee satisfaction among 400 health care organizations across the country.

Although other factors put into place alongside the Excellence Express initiative contributed to this morale boost, the senior staff believes that rewarding and recognizing outstanding behavior has led to a competition about who can do the best job, rather than who can do the least work. It has also created a unique culture in which employees have a reason to care about their jobs and the quality of their work.

A Word on Cost

Since initiating the program, SRHS has given out more than 1,800 Gold Spikes to its associates. This adds up to 9,300 Spikes that can be directly attributed to 9,300 acts of extraordinary service to patients or coworkers. SRHS has spent about $28,000 in trips to the tinderbox, but it typically spends $20,000 on turkeys at Thanksgiving each year—and managers and directors never quite know how many acts of extraordinary service each associate did to earn a turkey. Put into perspective, the money spent on the program isn't that much, especially because when SRHS managers say, "Great performances will be rewarded," associates know they're not talking turkey.

11

MANAGEMENT STYLE:
ZAG TO AVOID THE DRAG

Zig, zig, zig. Get through the daily routine. Make it to the weekend. Rely on what you know. Avoid uncertainties at all cost. Zigging is what you know and what you do.

Although you've promised yourself you'd never succumb to an ordinary, routine existence, that's what your work—and perhaps even your life—might have become. Beyond a morning latte, perhaps you no longer feel the need for a daily adrenaline rush. Indeed, you wonder if change is even your friend. Unless absolutely necessary, you don't want to rock the boat of predictability by infusing anything new or different into running your department or business.

After all, experience has taught you what works and what doesn't work. Within your organization, you've taken your experiences and transformed them into manuals, guidelines, rules, regulations, procedures, systems, and processes. You likely take comfort in predicting what comes next and know that if you stick to the plan, stay the course, do what works, and never go astray, then you'll make decisions that are safe.

Bam! Along comes a new breed of workers who completely upset the apple cart. They arrive in your employ prewired to interrupt your plans and destroy your processes without thinking twice. Quite obviously, they don't like following orders and certainly resist following anything that resembles a Standard Operating Procedure manual. You're now living the us-versus-them scenario described in Chapter 2.

Bore Them and They're Gone

Baby Boomers and Gen Xers are comfortable with plans, order, linear progression, and predictability. But this next generation finds all that boring. And if there's one thing the new crew can't stand, it's B-O-R-I-N-G. The sameness in which you might take comfort actually repels them. In fact, when surveyed, many young people respond that their fear of boredom in a job is greater than their fear of physical injury.

Such findings present a huge challenge for employers who need to fill routine jobs. It means that if you assign your kidployees to mundane positions or feed them a steady diet of routine tasks, you'll create a motivation gap between them and your desired outcome that rivals the Grand Canyon. You simply can't rely on a "zig" management style and expect to retain your young front-line staff—much less keep them motivated to perform at a high level. If you want them to give a damn about you or your business, it's time to become a master of the "zag."

Zag the Atmosphere

When I present staff development programs to elementary school teachers, I enjoy walking the halls and peering into the classrooms. Even when class isn't in session, it's easy to see what units and topics the children are studying just by looking around. If a class is studying Abraham Lincoln, for example, then I see pictures of President Lincoln on the classroom walls—from when he was a boy in a log cabin through his presidency and ultimate assassination. The pictures that surround the pupils visually depict the history they're learning.

Similarly, if the kids are studying how leaves vary from tree to tree, visitors not only see posters of leaves but the actual leaves that the teacher and the children have collected from nearby trees. Everywhere around them are colorful reading charts, reminders, schedules, and artwork. Knowing that the attention span of their pupils is short, teachers constantly change the environment to awaken and renew their sense of wonder. More than that, doing this keeps their pupils' minds on task.

However, if you walked into a high school classroom after the students have left for the day, you probably wouldn't know what topics are currently being discussed. You might not even be able to tell what subject is taught in that room. Somewhere between third grade and high school, teachers lose sight of how important it is to zag their learning environments. At this point, school becomes boring, and most students mentally check out.

Change the Wattage

Through its landmark Hawthorne Plant experiments conducted at the end of the industrial revolution, the Westinghouse company found that by increasing the wattage of the light bulbs in its factories, workers' productivity sharply increased. Curiously, when the company *decreased* the wattage, the productivity increased again. Researchers concluded that employee performance had little to do with the wattage of the light bulbs in the factories, but it had everything to do with employees' reactions to any sort of sensory stimulation.

Does This Pinpoint Your Challenge?

The solution becomes obvious—to vary your working environment continually. Inject a periodic zag into the atmosphere where your kidployees work. You can begin to develop a checklist for action by asking these questions:

- How long has it been since the break room in your organization has been repainted, remodeled, redecorated, etc?
- Are the safety posters on the wall due for an update?
- Are the vending machines dispensing anything new?
- Do the bathrooms smell fresh and clean or old and stale?
- Is there a current clipping or cartoon by the time clock?
- Would a change in the background music jazz things up?

Even casual Friday becomes boring when it's routine and predictable. Why not promote a formal Friday every now and then and have your kidployees wear their Sunday best. Or, if your dress code permits, announce you're having a "hat day" or a "concert t-shirt day" or a "wear your favorite team jersey" day. These kinds of ideas are fun, cost you

How do atmospherics in your workplace affect your employees' productivity? Even when you pay your front-liners well and give them incredible benefits, if their working environment doesn't occasionally get a facelift, these kidployees will get bored and mentally check out. If nothing around them ever changes, they'll view each day as a meaningless repeat of the previous day and feel as though they've been sentenced to purgatory. And you'll see their individual GAD factors decline.

nothing, and use your young employees' creativity to infuse a temporary visual change. Besides, they're considered cool.

Look carefully at your physical workplace surroundings. What sensory variables could you adjust to change the zig expectations of your front line into a zag experience that will rejuvenate them? Make a list of five things you can do to your atmosphere that would be new, exciting, or at least different.

> If it's been a while since you've mounted a new wall poster or changed the radio station, now is the time. If you haven't promoted a day when kidployees can forget the dress code, consider it. Whatever you do, don't stay the course. Throw a change-up pitch and catch 'em off guard.

Zag the Procedures

As a manager, you're probably more concerned with the end than the means. That's not a slam on you; that's your job. You're paid, promoted, and rewarded based on the bottom-line results you achieve. Your experience has led you to conclude that to get to X, you need to add A to B and multiply that by C. You're not trying to reinvent the wheel, for crying out loud; you just want to get to X— your desired outcome—the only way you know how.

Your kidployees also want to arrive at X. The problem occurs when they always have to add A to B and multiply by C day after day. That's when they'll check out. Your system will become their dungeon. They'll regard it as monotonous, predictable, routine, and yes . . . B-O-R-I-N-G.

You may be thinking, "But there's only one way to make a taco (bag groceries, apply a price tag, ring up a sale, etc.)." You recall that you had to achieve X when you were on the front line. Now, as a manager, you're expected to increase the speed and efficiency of getting to X while increasing quality and trimming costs. And there isn't just one X in your business; after all, you can't be in business in the new economy and have only one X. Odds are, you've got more Xs than you can handle, and you've got fewer resources than ever. Face it. You're pushed to the max. You're not only expected to do more with less, but even to do more with nothing!

This begs a few questions. Is there a better way to arrive at X? Is there a quicker way to arrive at X? Is there a more efficient way to arrive at X? If not, is there simply a different way to arrive at X? In short, how can you zag the procedure, to keep your front-liners happy and productive and still get to X?

Realize that even if a specific change you implement doesn't lead to significant results in itself, it still might prove beneficial if it stimulates the creative juices of your workforce. Taking away all variables could add comfort and ease for you, but it will turn them into robotic automatons. You'll get their bodies working for you, but their minds will disengage.

That's why it's imperative for you to experiment with new ways of getting to X—if not for the sake of productivity, then for the sake of retaining your front-line kidployees. If you assume only two roads lead to the promised land, see how you can find or create a third one, then a fourth and a fifth.

If you find yourself at a loss for implementing new ways to do old things, ask your kidployees. Even if they cannot think of a better system than the one you're using, they'll glow just knowing you valued their input enough to ask them. And as talented and technosavvy as this new breed of front-liner is today, don't be surprised if you discover a new procedure that saves both time and money while improving overall quality.

Zag the Outcome

Think back to when you were in your final years of high school. If you knew your folks would ground you for missing curfew, you'd do your best to get home on time. But if you were at a really great party that kept getting better as the night wore on—and you just met someone whom you had a huge crush on—you might conclude that getting grounded was an acceptable alternative to leaving the party on time.

Kidployees today are wizards at breaking your stride by applying the same reasoning. They know what happens if they show up late, if their cash drawer doesn't balance, or if they forget to remove their tongue ring before starting work. They also can reliably predict what type of compliment or reward awaits them for meeting or exceeding your standards. Unfortunately, predictability usually works against you. While it's important that your kidployees realize they face consequences for both good and poor performance, you can never allow them to think they've got you figured out.

What's the solution? Reenergize your young talent by occasionally confounding their expectations. Instead of giving your usual "good job" compliment, hand them movie passes or pull out your cell phone to call their parents and brag on their kid. Rather than shake your head when they show up late, put them on KP duty (like in the army) and have them clean the storeroom. These tactics take away their ability to predict what the outcome of their behavior will be. Good performance or bad performance, if you zag the outcomes, you'll keep their attention and their energy. Zagging usually registers a positive gain on their GAD scale.

Here's an example of zagging. The kid who doesn't wear the required necktie to work and knows he's going to get written up thinks, "Okay, this is my first violation, and I know the first offense is just a verbal warning. That will give me two more times before I get sent home and a report goes to the division headquarters. I've got a couple infractions to burn, so what the heck?"

What if, in this scenario, the kidployee knew about your "three strikes and you're out" rule but didn't know exactly what would happen during his first two strikes? If he knew he'd face some consequence for not wearing a necktie but didn't know what, he'd be less likely to play Russian roulette with your rulebook. Suppose that, on his first offense, you make him wear a really stupid-looking necktie—a dreadful "spare" you'd found at the secondhand store that you just happened to keep in your drawer for emergencies. Tell him the next time he shows up without a tie, you won't be so eager to "help him out" and that if he didn't like strike one, he surely won't like strike two. Now that you've zagged him once, he's probably unwilling to experiment with the unknown consequence of a second offense.

Remember, it's important to remain fair and equitable based on the nature of the kidployees' transgressions. You don't want to hit too hard with a first offense, or they might see you as a bully and develop a layer of insulation. Then again, you don't want to go too soft, or they'll see you as a pushover. If you're in doubt, take a few minutes of quiet time to sort it out before taking any punitive measures. Simply say to the offender, "I'm not real thrilled about what just happened, and we need to talk about it. I'll get with you in a little while."

Zag Works with Rewards, Too

You can zag the outcomes for negative behavior, and you'll want to do something similar for positive behaviors. If kidployees go above and beyond in their work assignments, reward them! But if they know what the reward is ahead of time and it's something they don't want or need, then they likely won't exert the extra effort to achieve it.

Suppose you tell a kidployee, "If you stay late tonight and make the front area of the store really shine, I'll give you two tickets to

When it comes to discipline, if they can predict what you're going to say or do, you lose the edge. And once you become predictable, some kidployees will play you for as long and hard as they can. Instead, if you can keep them off guard and uncertain about your next move, you tilt the playing field in your favor.

the game on Friday." You have made the assumption that the kid has no other plans on Friday and that the kid really wants to go to the game. In this case, the kid would probably give less than their best effort, believing it would be a waste because the kid doesn't care about the game.

However, if you say, "Do yourself a favor and really make this front area shine. If it takes you past quitting time, there's a nice little perk in it for you." That might be all the incentive the employees need to give it their best. If they met your expectations, you'd then present the game tickets with the understanding that, if the game wasn't going to work out, they could have something of equal value. The surprise element increases the perceived value of the perk. More than that, these employees will be looking for opportunities to impress you in the future.

"AT LEAST I'M NOT PREDICTABLE"

In the movie *Good Will Hunting,* Matt Damon played a blue-collar worker who has a brilliant mind. During a scene at a bar, Damon's character was competing against a Harvard student for the attentions of a young lady. The two got into a verbal scuffle, and the college man put him down in a particularly effective manner, but Damon's retort proved to be devastating. He simply said, "At least I'm not predictable."

Keep bobbing and weaving. Never be too predictable. When your front-liners get to the point where they're fully trained, when they have nothing new to learn and no changes to deal with from day to day, they might remain on your payroll, but their minds won't be focused on your business. And certainly if they get to the point of finishing your sentences for you, it's time to zag.

12

TURNOVER: SLOWING DOWN THE ENDLESS TREADMILL

Recruit, hire, train . . . quit. Recruit, hire, train . . . quit. As a business owner or manager of front-line staff, it might seem as if these four words sum up your job, or at least the lion's share of it. *You just can't find good people* is the second most frequently uttered phrase among managers, surpassed only by, *You just can't keep good people.*

Maybe you, too, feel like you're on the endless turnover treadmill (ETT), wondering if you'll ever find the stop button. The bad news is that no stop button exists; the good news is that you can control the speed at which it turns.

Even though you'll never completely eliminate turnover in your business, you can slow it down considerably and save an enormous amount of time and money in the process. Committing to employee retention *programs* isn't the answer because retention isn't a program—it's a process. A program is something you do; a process is something you never stop doing.

Roger Herman, noted author and employee retention guru, reminds us that retaining employees and developing a stable workforce involves a two-step process:

1. Understand why employees leave in the first place.
2. Develop and implement strategies to get them to stay.

Herman lists these five reasons why employees leave their jobs:

1. Poor working conditions
2. Lack of appreciation
3. Lack of support
4. Lack of opportunity for advancement
5. Inadequate compensation

Until the early 1970s, when people landed a job, they felt damned lucky. If their paychecks cleared at the end of the week, they'd report back to work on Monday. Back then, *company loyalty* wasn't an oxymoron. Workers felt a sense of allegiance to the company that gave them their daily bread. Obviously, the days of employee loyalty for loyalty's sake died and were buried with my leisure suit.

Now a job is a marriage, and both parties—the employer and the employee—need to be happy or one will file for divorce. The emerging workforce didn't create this situation; workers have had their eyes peeled for a bigger, better deal (BBD) for a long time. The new breed of kidployee is just quicker to demonstrate intolerance of working environments that are poor, inadequate, and lacking.

No Great Mystery

If you want to slow down the treadmill, look at things through the eyes of your kidployees. It's no great mystery why employees leave; Herman's research details it in the five simple reasons listed above. If you eliminate those reasons, you can greatly reduce turnover.

Therefore, the speed at which your kidployee turnover treadmill operates will be in direct proportion to your ability to reduce kidployees' thinking of their jobs as poor, inadequate, and/or lacking. If you continually strive to offer your front-liners the best possible working conditions, above average compensation, ample recognition, sincere appreciation, and a clear path to advancement, you can reduce costs substantially and get off the ETT.

Applying what you know about kidployees, here's how you can reverse Herman's five main reasons in your workplace:

1. Improve working conditions.
2. Show your appreciation.
3. Provide support.

4. Create avenues for advancement.
5. Offer better compensation.

IMPROVE WORKING CONDITIONS

Okay, you're not asking them to head down to the salt mines. But that doesn't mean they don't see work that way. If your front-liners think that they're being sent into battle without the arms they need to win, they will check out. Their tolerance is short for having to use old, antiquated equipment to do a job they know can be done in half the time with the right equipment. They won't continue to give their best when their working environment is too hot or too cold, too dark, too dangerous, too loud, or too anything.

A manager I know in the burger business was experiencing tumultuous turnover among the young front-liners in his restaurant. After interviewing a dozen of his former kidployees, he learned that almost two-thirds quit because the grill spattered grease over everything and ruined their clothes. Not knowing the specific reason for their discontent, he'd thought he just had to walk the treadmill. But when he discovered the primary reason, he invested in splatter guards for the grills and attired the front liners in a type of apron that protected their clothing and shoes from the grease. This slowed down the treadmill dramatically.

Inflexible scheduling is also a part of kidployees' definition of *poor working conditions*. New recruits often show up on the first day with a university degree and a bouquet of dreams but quickly are forced into a work routine that never seems to end. More and more young workers willingly forego higher earnings to achieve a suitable work-life balance. Companies that introduce work-life balance programs for their young workers find that turnover drops sharply and that these programs actually increase productivity.

Image is a huge factor with today's kidployees; they don't want their friends to think less of them because they have taken a lowly job or work in a dive. To keep them in your employ, therefore, make sure your front-liners know that management strives to create a pleasant and safe environment. While they might tolerate working conditions that are less than optimal, they won't tolerate a manager who knows the working conditions are poor and won't do anything about them.

FALLON WORLDWIDE

Fallon Worldwide is an advertising agency whose clients include Starbucks, Nikon, BMW, and Timex. Like many of the top firms in the advertising industry, the firm recruits some of the most clever, able, and creative young people available. These recruits quickly become accustomed to long hours and adopt a Zenlike devotion to the company and its clients.

Because stress, wavering creativity, and even burnout often plagued the careers of its promising stars, Fallon recognized the need to help refresh and revitalize them. The company introduced a program called Dreamcatchers, which provides time and funds to staff members who wish to travel or pursue a project. The program is available to employees who have been on board for at least three years.

In the first year, more than 50 employees took advantage of the program, some kayaking along the coast of South America, some running with the bulls in Spain, and others writing novels. Fallon's philosophy is that young people today want and need creative outlets. As one manager said, "We're a firm that lives by its wits. Creativity is what we must deliver to the marketplace, and we are always seeking ways to allow people to do their best work and to create cultural energy."

At Fallon, the cost of Dreamcatchers has been less than 1 percent of payroll, which the company regards as a bargain considering its highly favorable results. This program certainly goes a long way toward recruiting Opies and erasing the term *poor working conditions* from a kidployee's mind.

SHOW YOUR APPRECIATION

The ritual of trick-or-treating can be traced back centuries, when children donned handmade ceremonial costumes and went from door to door in their villages entertaining neighbors with songs, skits, and dances. If they performed well, the neighboring villager might reward them with bread, fruit, or nuts. Knowing that they would have to *do* something to *get* something pushed the kids to do their very best—that is, "a trick *for* a treat."

Today's youth simply aren't wired with a trick-*for*-treat mentality. They aren't even thinking trick-*or*-treat. They just want the treat: the bigger, the quicker, the simpler—the better. Further, they want to see the treat before they decide whether it's worth doing a trick for.

You might think that the only way to prevent your young employees from running to another job is to dole out new treats and keep their bags filled to the brim. Compensation is important to them, but perhaps the treat they value most isn't the one you have in mind.

We return to the old school versus new school approach to employee retention. The old school style of boosting salaries might still be effective with Boomers and perhaps even a few mature Xers, but it's an automatic disconnect with Gen Whys. To tap into their incredible potential, appeal to their "treat" mentality and always be ready to recognize, reward, and reinforce on the spot. Failure to do so will guarantee one result—your young talent will soon be doing the same trick for your competitors.

As a treat, money is sweet, but it's not sufficient in itself to attract, retain, and motivate good kidployees. Sure, they'll work for a paycheck, but they won't do their best work, and they certainly won't remain at the same job unless something more is present.

Appreciation is the greatest motivator in the world. Hunger for it is why we do what we do. Once basic needs are met, kidployees want to know that somebody notices them, accepts them, and acknowledges them. In the workplace, they might rent their bodies and minds to a third party, but it takes appreciation to touch their souls.

You Can't Fake It

You can con a con and you can fool a fool, buy you can't kid your kidployees into thinking you appreciate them when you really don't. And there will definitely be times when you don't! So the key is this: when you do appreciate your kidployees—for whatever reason—simply let them know.

One of the easiest ways to make certain you acknowledge your frontliners is to draw a simple grid. Down the left side, list the name of each person you supervise; across the top, list the days of the week. Then each time you say something positive to a kidployee, check the corresponding box beside their name. With a quick glance at a weekly chart, you'll see which kid might lack affirmation.

Also, develop an arsenal of openers to keep your praise relevant and specific to each person's actions. Here are some ideas to get you started:

- "I'm impressed with the way you . . ."
- "What a creative way to . . ."
- "Geez, you went all out when you . . ."
- "You really made a difference by . . ."
- "The reason you'll go far is . . ."
- "You've got to show the rest of the team how you . . ."

PROVIDE SUPPORT

Scott, a colleague of mine in the speaking business, has employed Nancy as his amazing administrative assistant for 13 years. The two work together like a well-oiled machine. When I pressed for his secret retention recipe, he said, "We simply try to make each other's live effortless and help each other reach our highest goals. The more I do for Nancy, the more she gives back. It's the ultimate win-win." Talk about support!

It's amazing how often employers misperceive the needs of their front-liners. It's a widely held belief that kidployees want to be left alone immediately after training and that they resist supervision and don't want to get close to their managers. But, actually, the opposite is true.

Your young talent wants to know they have your support, both personally and professionally. They want to know that you genuinely care for them and have their best interests at heart. But you can only support them by taking the time to get to know them. When you understand their goals and aspirations, you can help them achieve them—or at the very least, not stand in their way. And when they discover you're on their team, they won't want to leave yours.

The Third Leg of the Stool

Consider widening your base of support. After all, a stool with only two legs is not much good, but when you add a third leg, you can sit on it with confidence. In this case, the parents of your kidployees comprise the additional leg.

If at all possible—and only if you have done your homework to ensure this is appropriate and fitting—introduce yourself to the parents of your new hire. Even busy parents want to know how well their kids are doing and what they're learning at work. They also like knowing who's teaching their kid how to work and what kind of management philosophy or leadership style is in place.

A simple phone call to say that you're glad to have Allison on board makes a strong favorable impression. Invite her parents into your place of business to get acquainted. Offer to meet them for a cup of coffee, and the positive impact will be even greater. When you do meet them, make sure you exchange contact information, as it can certainly come in handy later.

In addition to informing her parents about their daughter's performance and growth, extend Allison's employee discount to them as a gesture of goodwill. Later, if Allison tells her dad she might look for a new job, chances are he'll encourage her to stay put. Although it's a small thing, the discount might be the tipping point that keeps the legs of the stool firmly in place.

Support can take many forms. The more time you invest in getting to know your front-liners, the more likely you'll hit on the kind of support that resonates with them. And as research proves, if you support them, they will support you.

CREATE EXCITING AVENUES FOR ADVANCEMENT

It doesn't take Scooby Doo to figure out why so many companies have a tough time slowing down their ETT. Young people know that the key to their growth lies in the combination of training and experience that they can add to their résumé. They view degrees as a dime a dozen. They realize that only training from their job will carry weight in the eyes of future employers, so they depend on their work for continual growth and development. But most jobs, particularly entry-level ones, are so narrowly defined that opportunities to broaden their experience are few and far between.

Managers, especially in large corporations, rarely open up to the idea of allowing their kidployees a chance to move off the front line and try something different. The way they see it, they hired them for the front line, so they should be happy and thankful for the chance to serve.

But if you've got an Opie on your payroll, that kid won't stay long unless challenged. In fact, even an average kidployee won't stay immobile

Smart employers keep finding new ways to keep their top performers on a growth track and off the treadmill. Taking steps as simple as including a kidployee in a management meeting and giving them a chance to participate or introducing her to important contacts in your network give that young worker the sense that they're learning, moving, and developing.

long before checking out—either quitting or shifting into cruise mode. Providing an environment that offers continuous opportunities to grow and learn through frequent changes in roles, responsibilities, and projects builds a sense of loyalty in young talent. Don't lose sight of that.

C *a s e* S *t u d y*

CRACKER BARREL

Cracker Barrel restaurants, a major employer of youth, has a program designed to keep kidployees growing. Turnover in the restaurant industry is well over 100 percent, but for hourly workers who have completed all four parts of Cracker Barrel's Personal Achievement Responsibility (PAR) training program, turnover is down to 24 percent.

Every new Cracker Barrel restaurant employee has the option of entering the PAR program. Those who do so typically want to maximize their employment experience. They begin as a PAR 0. Throughout the PAR training, they learn and practice a growing set of skills, from the basics of the job to leadership and conflict resolution. They take written tests and are evaluated by managers. To progress through the program, workers must earn increasingly higher grades. The program is offered in English and Spanish, and the company pays workers to study written learning materials.

As the young workers progress through PAR I, PAR II, and so on, they earn salary raises and larger company contributions toward incentives, including health insurance and greater discounts on store purchases. In more recent years, PAR IV employees have been able to participate in a separate internship program, which grooms in-store workers to become associate store managers on a management track. The only educational prerequisite is a high school diploma or the equivalent.

High turnover typical in the restaurant industry can seriously erode the profitability of an otherwise successful concept. The PAR program is one reason that Cracker Barrel has been the top performing chain in its category for 13 consecutive years. When you actively work to grow your front line, your front-liners will work to grow your business.

OFFER BETTER-THAN-AVERAGE COMPENSATION

Suppose you're offered more money to work for another company. Even if you turn it down to stay where you are, I bet you listened to the offer before you declined it. The amount you're paid for what you do is important to you, so you look for opportunities that might bring in more money.

Your young talent approaches new opportunities exactly the same way.

Although earning money isn't the only reason kidployees work, and it might not even be their most important reason, it's still high on their list. The amount they're paid indicates their market value and serves as a measure of how well they're doing compared to their friends. In addition, it helps them negotiate for what they want.

Anyone who believes that post-Generation Xers aren't materialistic doesn't have kids. Pop culture has shown them that status and stuff go hand in hand. While the cost of living has jumped, the cost of living *well* has soared. Your front-liners have seen what money will buy—and they want in.

Waving Bigger Bucks

Unless you've completely eliminated the other four reasons that employees might leave your company, you have no margin of error with this one. You simply can't offer average wages and keep an above-average kid on your payroll. Because your competitor is waving bigger bucks to lure them away, it's critical that you put a solid compensation strategy in place.

While you might be able to fish low-end talent out of the pool using minimum-wage bait, landing keepers (like Opie) is trickier. Even though they're relatively new to the workforce, they already know the score and are comparison shopping. You can cut to the chase simply by outspending your competitors and paying a wage no one else can match, or you can offer a package that offers a competitive wage but is also loaded with cool perks. Your goal is to ensure they choose you.

What's in it for you? By increasing the average time that front-line workers stay on staff by even a month or two, you'll enjoy a greater peace of mind, higher profitability, and less time on the turnover treadmill.

While most kidployees won't become managerial staff, McDonald's Corporation, still the world's largest restaurant chain, offers its long-term employees a smorgasbord of benefits. These include credit union membership, daycare, 401(k) accounts, and expanded health insurance benefits. Individual franchise owners are empowered to extend these corporate benefits to their employees in addition to any benefits that they offer locally.

Most of the fast-food chains also offer tuition reimbursement programs. They encourage workers who want to attend college to return as managers at some point. Certainly, many universities are populated by students whose fast food employers have helped foot the bill for them to earn a degree.

Demonstrate Mastery

It makes sense to tie compensation to contribution. The more a kid can contribute, the more they should make. A client of mine in the grocery business raises the hourly wage of its kidployees when they demonstrate mastery in 21 different key areas. For example, new hires start at minimum wage but can get an instant raise of $.15 an hour by demonstrating they can sweep and mop floors to store standards. They can get another $.10 an hour when they score 100 percent on a quiz listing the exact location of 30 grocery items.

> Compensation isn't only what you give employees; it's also what you don't take from them. It's to your advantage to make your products and services ridiculously affordable—if not free—to your kidployees. Odds are, they want to work for you because they have a passion for what you make or sell.

When designing a compensation strategy around retention, consider offering retroactive raises. Many of the White Castle restaurants have motivated new hires to stay by promising automatic raises that go back to their start date. The raise—typically $.50 an hour—kicks in anywhere from 30 days to 3 months after they start work, depending on the manager's discretion. This strategy is particularly effective when managers want to encourage seasonal help to remain throughout the year.

A kid paid $6 an hour might stay on at an electronics store because they can buy stereo equipment at a 50 percent discount rather than jumping to a supermarket that pays $7 an hour. My 20-year-old son stayed on as a cook in his college dorm for a lower wage than he could have made doing landscaping, simply because he got all of his meals free. Remember, your kidployees will remain with a company if they believe they're getting a better-than-average deal compared to their other options.

FIND THE PAUSE BUTTON

Two things are required to get off the Endless Turnover Treadmill:

1. Know why employees leave.
2. Set up comprehensive strategies to eliminate those reasons.

As one manager stated, you can't treat retention as a policy or a program; it's an ongoing, multipronged process that encompasses all areas of management.

In essence, retaining kidployees depends on factors such as how they're hired, the kind of work they do, how they're paid and promoted, what constitutes grounds for dismissal, the challenges they're given, the opportunities for learning, and whether they're made to feel part of a team.

Keep these vital axioms about retention in mind:

- Kidployees don't quit companies; they quit managers.
- Kidployees know getting another job, another manager, and new training is a hassle; they don't have that much thirst for change.
- Kidployees will put up with the pain of change if it means they can escape a bad relationship.
- Kidployees will leave if they find out that their wages are distinctly lower than what they can get elsewhere. They're not necessarily materialistic, but they do value certain goods and certain brand names. And they want to be paid well for their time.

In this day and age of near-zero corporate loyalty, retention doesn't happen automatically. It takes a combination of effective programs and meaningful approaches that include the following:

- Getting support from parents
- Offering exciting avenues for advancement
- Providing recognition, rewards, time off, and creative perks

As in all other areas of management, you can't do just one of these and expect amazing results. You'll find the magic in the mix!

HOW TO CONNECT WITH THEM

Because Getting Them
to Give a Damn Is an Inside Job

13

ORIENTATION AND TRAINING: BUY IN FROM DAY ONE

Growing up in Colorado, I had a lot of buddies who learned to ski before they could walk. My parents didn't have a lot of money for recreational pursuits, so my first skiing experience didn't come until I was a junior in high school and I had saved up enough money to pay for the lift ticket myself.

My father didn't believe in the concept of renting equipment and told me that, if I was going to take up skiing, he'd buy me everything I needed. After an $18 shopping spree at the Goodwill Store down the street, Dad had crossed out everything on his list: skis, boots, poles, and clothing. My equipment looked like something out of a bad cartoon, but my ski outfit looked even worse. When my buddies pulled up outside my house to pick me up on a cold January morning, I loaded up my equipment in the car and begged them to quit laughing.

When we arrived at the Winter Park ski area, my friends were more than a little amused as I laced up the leather boots and attached them via cable bindings to my seven-foot, wooden Army skis. They helped me onto the chairlift, and we headed up the mountain toward the double-black diamond runs (which they cruelly told me were the beginner runs). Once we arrived at the top, they took off down the slopes like Olympic hot-doggers, leaving me all alone to fend for myself.

Needless to say, my baptism into the world of skiing was one of the hardest, most painful days of my young life. It's a miracle I ever went back.

A new hire's first day on a job can be a lot like that. Predictably, it's among the most stressful experiences they endure. Regardless of how calm and together they appear on the outside, odds are they arrive nervous, jittery, and full of self-doubt. They might not have the right attire or the required equipment (paperwork, tools, money for lunch, etc.). To complicate matters, they don't know anyone and must remember myriad names, faces, positions, and more. They want to impress you but could be so intimidated that they can't remember even the simplest of tasks. It's not baptism by fire; it's baptism by flamethrower!

GO FOR AN EARLY VICTORY

To increase your odds of getting kidployees to give a damn about you, your business, and your customers, pull out all the stops to make their first day a banner day. Make a concerted effort to welcome them, reaffirm their decision to work in your business, and encourage them in any training or task they undertake. Use affirmations like, "You've obviously got a knack for this business!", "You're going to love working here because . . .", "I know I made the right choice hiring you, because . . .", and, "You picked this up a lot quicker than most . . ."

> Throwing kidployees on the front line the day they arrive is akin to sending soldiers into battle before they know how to pull the trigger on their gun. Feeling on guard, they fervently wish to avoid being humiliated, made to feel stupid, or otherwise put down. On their first day, many new hires conclude that the job isn't right for them, so they put up a shield and develop a negative attitude that they carry throughout their tenure.

On the first day, the key is to make them feel as if they've got the right stuff for the job, they've found a home, and they'll be a part of something great. You also want them to know that you genuinely like them and have faith in them; you certainly want them to feel comfortable to come to you with questions or concerns. When they go home and are asked, "How did your first day go?" you want them to respond, "Very cool job. I'm gonna love working there!"

Although it was more than 30 years ago, I still vividly remember my first day at the Pagoda Restaurant. Don Wong made sure I knew that I was an idiot, he was the boss, and I was a lowly slave. I wasn't there to have fun, he didn't want to get to know me beyond work, and he'd be watching my every move. After that introduction, it would have taken three weeks of his praising me nonstop for me to have changed my first impression of the job, let alone for me to give a damn about his business.

It shouldn't be that way for your new recruits. Commit yourself to be that one-employer-in-a-million who gets your kidployees excited out of the starting blocks and keeps them yearning to learn and develop new skills throughout their employment. Here's how.

Begin with an Orientation, Not Skills Training

Many companies believe they are beginning with an orientation, when all they're really doing is making a few introductions and then launching into a physical training session. "Let me show you where we keep the supplies" is not the kind of orientation I'm discussing. Although it's necessary to know logistical things before starting the actual job, logistics won't calm your new hire's nerves. Such a start could even make them more anxious, wondering if they'll be able to remember coworker's names and where everything is kept. Instead, remember the three Cs of an effective orientation: take steps to make your rookies feel comfortable, confident, and capable before they begin actual training.

Despite my horrific first day skiing as a teen, I was determined to learn. I started going to the ski slopes alone to practice until I finally got good enough to keep up (just barely) with my buddies. I had saved my money to buy a car, but spent some of it on good used ski equipment. Within a few months, I had developed a passion for the sport.

Decades later, when my children were in grade school, I introduced them to skiing using a more conventional approach. With the right equipment and professional instruction, Zac and Whitney were skiing intermediate runs within a few days. However, when they reached the eighth grade, they each traded in their skis for a snowboard, which they thought to be much hipper and cooler than skis.

I soon faced the reality that my kids would be going off places on their snowboards that I couldn't follow. So, after 26 years of skiing, I, too, made the switch. Experts will tell you it takes an adult three full days of lessons—and lots of bumps and bruises—to get comfortable on a snowboard. But I didn't want to invest three whole days looking like a newbie and feeling like an oldie. Besides, I had gone down that road once during my teens and I didn't want to travel it a second time. I committed myself to the extreme sport of snowboarding in a quest to shave two days off the predicted learning curve.

I started by buying the right snowboard equipment and practiced putting on and taking off my board in my living room. I then watched several hours of instructional video to learn what snowboarding was all about. I asked my kids to explain the general idea to me and to tell me what to expect. When I got to the slopes, I stood at the base of the mountain and carefully observed some really good boarders. When they got back in the lift line, I asked questions and solicited advice. By the time I strapped on my snowboard, I knew exactly what to expect. I felt comfortable, confident, and capable—and it worked! Before day's end, I'd become a boarding fool catching some major-league air. *I was in a zone and locked on, dude.*

Assess What They Know

Rarely will a kidployee arrive at your workplace armed with the skill set necessary to perform well in the capacity for which they were hired. While this isn't exactly news to any manager employing younger workers, what makes this new breed so different is that they can also lack even the fundamental foundation needed to learn your company's basic skills.

What is incredibly perplexing to managers, especially training managers, is the paradox between their new hire's lack of basic skills and their incredible technology and business savvy. No, these aren't kids who set up a lemonade stand for their first business. Many of them trade stock online and have learned to trade well. Even more have their own credit cards. While today's new front-line employees might not know the basics of supply and demand or even dollars and cents, they have tremendous personal experience with marketing, public relations, new product launches, market research, and advertising.

> By spending time up front getting to know your recruits, you'll establish the personal relationship necessary to coach them. You'll also be able to identify the attitudes and values that need to be reinforced as well as the skills that need to be trained. At the same time, you'll make sure you set up a firm foundation of understanding for that coaching.

Showing a video of your company's history and philosophies to your new hires isn't the best way to begin training. Not only will it bore them to tears, it will also begin a process of singled-sided communications, because it says, "Here's our company, here's our founder, here's our world headquarters, here's our mission, here's what others say about us, blah, blah." Granted, it's important for employees eventually to learn about your company and why it's been successful. But for openers, it's much better to find out who they are, what their personal stories are, and what they know about life.

Continually Reinvent Your Training

If it's been more than six months since you updated your training materials, they could easily be obsolete. While the methodologies and procedures might not have changed, the language and the examples probably have. If the goal is to arm your front-liners with the skills necessary to perform capably in any circumstance or condition, then you'll have to keep them engaged throughout the training to make certain they absorb the information. To keep them engaged, it's critical to continually update, modify, and revamp your training materials.

When it comes to the content in your training modules and materials, be leery of aiming for the lowest common denominator. If you use simple language designed for a 12-year-old, you'll pander to your underachievers while making your potential Opies roll their eyes in agony. It's also important to review your existing materials to see what might be overstated or no longer valid. Look for anything that can be trimmed, edited back, and condensed.

To summarize, take out the arcane, the outdated, and the inapplicable. If you're unsure what material is fresh and relevant, solicit input from your top-achieving kidployees. Instruct them to go through the training materials from the perspective of a young trainee and ask for their feedback.

Know that your trainees are chomping at the bit to show the world what they can do. That's why you don't want to tie them up in training for an extended period. You'll have to wrestle with the question: "Do kids have to know everything before they can do anything?" Admittedly, many training modules offer too much at once. Do yours?

If you force kidployees to endure the entire training manual before turning them loose on the job itself, you'll experience a low rate of retention and a high error rate, guaranteed. Their shorter attention spans call for shorter training sessions. Experiment. It might work to your advantage to teach your

As they demonstrate mastery, compliment them on doing the task well and move on to a new skill using the same formula. A colleague of mine who is a professional skills trainer refers to this as the "stick and move" method and says it is, by far, the most effective way to train today's kidployees.

new hires a specific skill, test them on it, and then put them on the front line to practice it under supervision. Later, allow them to perform the skill unsupervised.

Where to Turn for Answers

Mistakes in your workplace can prove costly, but the ones that drive you nuts are those that you know could have been avoided if the kidployee had "just asked a manager for help."

When engaged in the training process, you see how they soak up information like sponges. But because they feel self-conscious about appearing successful and competent, they feel embarrassed if they don't know how to answer a question or solve a problem. So instead of asking for help, they act on impulse instead of reason—and can leave a big mess in their wake.

For this reason, it's imperative that you communicate to your front-liners exactly where to find answers to common problems. "No question is a bad question" is always a good policy to establish. Like most people, they'll feel more comfortable when openly encouraged to ask for help. However, when a manager isn't available to answer questions, they need to know where and how to access key information.

Round Table Pizza, one of the largest pizza chains in the western United States, reduced its training manual for front-line kidployees to the size of a Game Boy. The training department created and dispersed a graphically enhanced, tabbed, and laminated spiral bound book that young people find easy to use. Now any kidployee working in any area of the restaurant can reach into their back pocket, pull out the manual, and quickly find the needed step-by-step instruction. As a result of having this manual on hand, Round Table managers have seen a significant reduction in mistakes and aren't pestered with trivial questions that can be answered easily by checking the manual.

Don't Just Train the *What;* Train the *Why*

"I'll have a hot apple pie and a vanilla shake," the customer said. The kidployee at the fast food restaurant who took his order replied, "Fine, sir. Would you like any dessert with that?" My colleague Nido Qubein, a professional speaker and chairman of Great Harvest Bread Company, shared this amusing anecdote to illustrate how young employees are uniformly trained on how to "reply" but not educated on how to "relate." Sad but true.

Indeed, many managers and supervisors get so caught up in the rigid training of their young employees that they forget to educate them. They teach the *how-to* but not the *why* behind a procedure. Consequently, kidployees might know *what* to do, even when they don't have the foggiest notion *why* they are doing it. This kind of cut-to-the-chase training enables front-liners to blurt out a properly formatted response to predetermined questions, but when the formula is tampered with, even slightly, the results can be alarming.

> Although kidployees can be the worst learners if they don't see relevance in the subject matter, you'll find them among the best learners when they see personal benefit in the lesson. This means that your training strategy needs to play to the ever-questioning mindset of your emerging workforce.

Once the thrill of getting the new job and being trained for it wears off, your new kidployees most likely become bored with the day-to-day reality of work. That's when they really start to question your procedures and processes, asking questions like, "Why do I need to learn that?", "What is the point of smiling?", and "Isn't there a short cut to doing this?" If they're not asking these questions verbally, they're doing it mentally. They want to learn, but if the learning process isn't entertaining enough or if they don't deem it important or applicable, they'll check out.

On the opposite end of the spectrum, kidployees look toward the future and are extremely eager to amass the cutting-edge skills that will increase their job-market value.

Never take for granted that your kidployees understand the importance of the skill you're teaching them. Clearly state the reason they need to know what you're about to teach them and how that new tool will benefit them on the front line. When they see that the training gives them a tool for feeling more successful, they'll buy in to the necessary training.

Keep Training Fun, Interactive, and Engaging

If the training you offer rates low on the fun-o-meter, you won't be able to break through your kidployees' mental barriers and inject your message. Kidployees will simply tune out and shut down, because they're used to getting their information with high-speed graphics and an adrenalin rush. Realize that many of their classes at school are project based and fun driven; that's what they know. The onus is on you to provide training materials that teach core concepts and necessary skills in a fun and entertaining way. That criteria is especially critical when hiring presenters to come in as part of their training.

> Be conscious of your new hires' propensity for multitasking and allow them the flexibility to progress at a high rate of speed. While moving through training too fast might confuse them, going too slowly will lull them to sleep—and confusion is more easily remedied than boredom.

How do you increase the fun factor? Certainly make sure they aren't sitting idle listening to a talking head. If they're not involved at all, they're not having fun and they're certainly aren't learning. Today's employees are too multisensory to absorb much information from lecture-only education. For success, every aspect of training must invite them to jump in. If they can't be the pilots of their own training, at least let them be the copilots. In situations that require classroom lecture style, make certain your young trainees have the freedom to ask questions the second they come to mind instead of holding them to the end of an instructor's monologue. That makes them feel more involved.

Research tells us that every eight minutes, your kidployees disengage from lecture-based instruction, no matter how good the instructor is. Television has programmed their minds to absorb content for a maximum of eight minutes before a commercial break. That's why it's imperative to involve them, change techniques, or give them a mental break at least seven times in an hour. Failure to do so invites low retention.

IN THE FINAL ANALYSIS

If you want to connect your front line with your bottom line, your kidployees need to feel that they are learning and growing. They want to believe they're important contributors and an asset to you. Of course, they can only be as good as their skills allow them to be—and their skills will be as good as you train them to be.

Applying the six considerations discussed in this chapter is instrumental in training your kidployees to function at their highest possible level. Review the following six considerations often, and make sure you're implementing them every day:

1. Begin with an orientation.
2. Assess what they know.
3. Continually reinvent your training.
4. Let them know where to turn for answers.
5. Don't just train the *what;* train the *why.*
6. Keep training fun, interactive, and engaging.

14

COMMUNICATION: LAYING DOWN THE LAW AND KEEPING IT

"**I**t's my way or the highway."

I heard that statement a lot in my first jobs. I also heard it from my parents, teachers, and coaches. Naturally, when I left teaching and got into management, I said it a fair amount to my young charges. It just seemed the natural thing to say to show them who was boss. I certainly didn't want my subordinates to question my power. I believed that being "feared and revered" was the only way I could stay in control—and I was terrified of not being in control. For the most part, the my way/highway strategy seemed to work in the '80s and early '90s. But those days are gone.

Say, "It's my way or the highway," to your subordinates today, and you'll stare at a lot of taillights heading toward the highway. If the use of a worn-out cliché doesn't immediately turn them off, then the arrogant assertion of power will. It's not that they get put off by structure and shy away from discipline. To the contrary, as you'll see in this chapter, some of the most successful employers of young talent attract the best and brightest *because* they have rigid rules and zero tolerance for deviation. However, exerting power and control for control's sake will no longer work; in fact, it's an open invitation to disaster.

FIRM POLICIES IN PLACE

To maintain order and ensure productivity and profit, your organization has put in place firm rules, policies, and procedures. These need to be communicated to your kidployees. And, unless you're the sole owner of your company, odds are you didn't make the rules. You might not like these rules or agree with them, but as a manager or supervisor, you do have to enforce them.

Your kidployees want to know what you expect of them, and—just like you when you entered the workforce—they're dying to know what rules they can get away with breaking. You can try to be their buddy, but sooner or later, you'll have to "lay down the law." That's why it's advantageous to clearly articulate the rules—particularly those that have proven to be the hardest to enforce—in the early going, perhaps before training begins. You don't want to surprise new hires by laying out the rules of the road while they're on it.

It's a good idea to avoid throwing a long list of dos and don'ts at your new recruits on the first day. Find the fine line between sharing important ground rules at the right moment and freaking them out by having them sign a lengthy employee conduct agreement. However, if your company policy doesn't allow them to have exposed tattoos, or you have a no-smoking policy, or you require them to attend an employee meeting every Saturday at 7:00 AM, you'd be wise to point out these tidbits in the initial interview. They could be deal busters.

WHAT ARE THEY BUYING INTO?

You want your kidployees to buy in, so they need to know what they're buying into. Remember, they're not opposed to structure, and they do appreciate knowing where the boundaries are. You'll have an easier time laying down the law—and a much easier time upholding it—if kidployees recognize that your rules are

1. fair,
2. relevant,
3. consistent, and
4. enforced.

Let's analyze these four descriptors first, then see how they apply to laying down the law for common employee problems.

Fair

The most commonly spoken phrase by adolescents in America is, "That's not fair!" If you have kids, you know this is all too true. Therefore, the only way to get your young talent to respect your rules is for those rules to be perceived as fair.

What's a fair rule? It's one to which they respond with, "Oh, yeah, I can see why that makes sense." Knowing that a rule has been put in place for a valid reason makes all the difference in how they respect it, even if they don't show respect outwardly. It's their nature to question why they're being asked to adhere to a standard, so take time to show them the value of the rule you want them to live with—and how it's ultimately in their best interests to follow it.

Clarity is another measure of fairness. Let your front-liners know exactly what behavior is acceptable and what won't be tolerated. Don't leave anything to interpretation (or misinterpretation). Can they sample the goodies? To whom can they extend their employee discount? If they try on that new denim jacket, can they continue to wear it on the floor while helping customers? What should they do if they can't get to work? Simply stated, ensure that your rules are easy to understand and that every employee reads and signs off on them. Then make certain you've clearly defined the consequences for disobeying these rules. Review your rules to ensure they're impartial but not inflexible. Of course, you need to uphold high standards, but also expect a degree of variance or you'll end up in an asylum. In your quest to be fair and equitable, don't make the mistake of treating everyone exactly the same. I call this "political correctness run amok." Besides, in practical life, fairness simply doesn't work that way. Dispense discipline with an even hand, but build in a margin of flexibility to allow for individuality.

Relevant

It's their nature to question why (hence *Generation Why*, the term I coined for post-Gen Xers). It's next to impossible to enforce a rule that has no business being on the books. Yet many organizations spend inordinate amounts of time doing just that!

Supervisors in one company I consulted with felt frustrated because their kidployees wouldn't follow the policy of no facial piercings (other than earlobes). While this rule has relevance in a hospital setting, the kidployees affected were doing data entry during graveyard hours. They were only seen by each other and a supervisor. To them, the rule was irrelevant. One 19-year-old told me, "Look, if I wanted to interface with the public, I wouldn't be working the night shift. I took this job because I can keyboard at warp speed and I don't want someone standing over me or telling me what to wear. If I do my job, that's all that matters."

Effective managers keep their rulebooks light and tight. They continually delete unnecessary items, leaving only those policies and procedures for which they have a solid rationale and won't grant any leeway. This makes the remaining rules easier to remember, justify, and enforce.

Do your best to rid your policy manual of any rules established to exert power and control over your front-line staff. Take a highlighter to your rulebook and mark only the rules that are absolutely necessary. Then get out your scissors and start trimming away the fat.

Consistent

While it's important to have *some* flexibility in *some* situations, it's far better to err on the side of consistency. Make certain that the consequences for breaking major company rules (theft, chronic absenteeism, and so on) are automatic and nondiscretionary. This keeps you from playing good cop/bad cop and allows you to maintain your impartiality. If kidployees see older workers and managers bending the rules, they'll regard the rules as arbitrary and assume that they, too, can bend some rules. There's nothing dicier than calling kidployees on a rule violation and having them retort, "But I see you doing it all the time!"

If you say you will do something, do it. Never allow your front-liners see you go back on your word or make a special exception for a "pet" employee. They'll respect you—and your rulebook—much more if they know no one gets a pass. Being consistent means the rules apply to everyone.

Never compromise on your rules and standards for the sake of filling positions or wanting to come across as a cool person. Once your front-liners get a whiff of soft leadership, a lack of ethics or standards, or any hint of incongruity, you've lost their respect and their buy in. Trying to win back either of these is a Herculean task.

Enforced

I live in a mountain community where no fences are allowed. Our house sits on two acres surrounded by neighbors on all sides. We have a golden retriever named Tucker who loves to run and explore, but we don't want him to invade the privacy of our neighbors. We can't stomach the thought of chaining him to a post, so we invested in an invisible fence—a thin, buried wire that encircles the property and carries a mild electrical current.

The wire works in concert with a transmitting collar we put around Tucker's neck. When he gets within ten feet of the wire, he hears a beeping noise. As he gets closer, the frequency of the beeping noise accelerates. If he ignores the warning and crosses the barrier, he immediately receives a mild shock that reminds him he's gone too far. The shock sends him back inside the ten-foot boundary and conditions him to respect the beep. We've learned that this system works about 98 percent of the time.

> In reality, your rules are only as good as your ability to enforce them. If you allow your kidployees to break through defined barriers without experiencing a consequence, you condition them and their coworkers to continue that behavior—just as if Tucker didn't have that electric fence to enforce his boundary. As difficult as doling out a "shock" might be, you must be willing to do so.

However, if we fail to recharge Tucker's collar at least once a week, it loses its power. Occasionally a deer, elk, fox, or even a skunk runs by our property. Naturally, Tucker wants to give chase and just takes off. We've learned that if the beep doesn't sound, he'll take off for hours. Whenever that happens, it then takes a long, long time to retrain him to respect the boundaries.

THREE IMPORTANT RULES

#1: Be Likeable

You don't have to be your kidployees' best friend, but always be friendly. They feel an allegiance toward a boss they respect and genuinely like. When asked why they don't pilfer, lie to their boss, call in sick to get a day off, or fudge on the timesheet, kidployees often say something like, "She's a really cool lady, and I wouldn't want to do anything to hurt or disappoint her." Ironically, if you're perceived as being fair and consistent in enforcing relevant rules, they will like you and look up to you with a great deal more reverence than if you aren't fair or consistent. They know you have a job to do; they simply want to think of you as a person with a heart, a soul, and a conscience.

#2: Build In an Element of Fun

A spoonful of medicine helps the sugar go down, right? It's far easier to enforce rules and discipline when your kidployees are allowed to have some fun—and perhaps some organized chaos—in the workplace.

When I worked in a clothing store during high school, my coworkers and I loved it when the manager left the premises. That's when we'd start throwing straight pins to pop the balloons on display. Or we'd dress up in new clothes (price tags still on) and pose as mannequins in the mall windows, then wait until people walked up to the glass and startle them. Or we'd lie on an outdoor sidewalk sale table covered with marked-down pants. When someone walked up to the table, we'd pop out from underneath the pile, hold up a pair of pants, and say, "This one might fit!"

Yeah, working in that men's store, we sure got our kicks from freaking people out. We wanted to have fun—and fun was a no-no back then. Bosses went out of their way to suppress any type of horseplay that kidployees might have. Work was supposed to be strictly business and "by the book." Most appealing for us was creating our own fun by throwing out the rulebook.

Your kidployees shouldn't have to break your rules to have fun. Be proactive about it. Instead of only laying down the don'ts, lay down the dos as well. Let them know what kind of horseplay you allow and when. Structure the chaos. When fun at work is no longer the forbidden fruit, you'll have a much easier time getting buy in for your rulebook.

#3: Reverse-Discipline Your Rule Followers

Instead of instituting a consequence for when your front-liners break the rules, why not reward them for following the rules? Instead of, "Three strikes and you're out," try, "Hit the safe zone and watch cool things happen!" Don't confuse this strategy with having a recognition and reward program for outstanding performance; these rewards are simply a technique to get 16- to 24-year-old employees to play by your rules.

My daughter attended a high school that had a very strict dress code. Whitney, a fashion princess, always wanted to push the dress code to the limit. Then she learned that students who made it through an entire semester without a code violation could opt out of a final exam from any class of their choosing. That's all it took; she never again pushed the dress code boundaries. Taking the final exam wasn't a punishment, but *not* having to take it was certainly an incentive—not for achieving excellence, but for obeying the rules. Whitney bought in to that.

Whoa! Stop and think of how this technique could work for you. Imagine, for example, that instead of paying your front-liners $6.75 an hour, you paid them $6.50 an hour with a stipulation that, every month, if their personnel record was free of dress code infractions, they'd receive a 25-cent bonus retroactive to the first day of the month. You'd be rewarding them for adhering to the code (pleasant and fun for both of you) rather than punishing them for *not* adhering to the code (unpleasant and not fun for either of you).

You can find ways to make this idea work in a number of different scenarios, depending on your industry and specific concern. Offer a premium for good attendance and punctuality, instead of threatening them when they're late or absent. Or offer an incentive for turning in a cash drawer that balances instead of taking money out of their paychecks when their drawers don't balance. You'll find you can eliminate three or four of your biggest challenges with your front-liners just by taking a reverse-discipline approach.

KIDPLOYEE DRESS CODES AND APPEARANCE

No single topic I cover in my programs is more hotly debated and agonized over than this one—appearance. It's worthy of its own book, but I'll cut to the chase and summarize what I've learned from managers and today's kidployees.

In some companies, perhaps yours, having your image represented professionally to the public is critical to your success. Yet what front-liners wear can be a source of consternation. Managers and supervisors frequently grieve under their breath, "I can't stand what these kids are wearing today. It's driving me nuts. I'm signing their paychecks and this is my store, so you'd think they'd at least *try* to meet me in the middle. But they're coming in here with tattoos, piercings, hip-huggers, and hats turned backwards. Half of them look like pimps and prostitutes, and it seems like the others just want to piss me off."

My first response is always, "Are your appearance expectations clearly established up front? Have your front-liners bought in to your established dress code?" You see, you never want to get into syntax problems, and you certainly don't want to force them to wear something in which they're not comfortable. With image being so vitally important to them,

> Determine at the outset whether a candidate for your front-line position is willing to don the right clothes. You can head off 90 percent of future problems by establishing clear expectations from the get-go. Only hire those who are willing to play the part; avoid those who aren't.

it's easier to push a string across a table than it is to get kidployees to buy in to a dress code they consider to be totally dorky.

What It Means to Dress Professionally

So if you say to kidployees, "We want you to dress professionally," what you define as *professional* could be entirely different from what *professional* means to them. Instead, you have to outline—sometimes to the nth degree—exactly what you mean by "professional or appropriate dress."

In addition to stating your code in precise, can't-misinterpret language, provide photographs showing how one should properly wear the uniform and groom for work. Provide a second set showing unacceptable attire and grooming. Then spend time explaining to your recruits the reasons behind your standards. If you do this, you'll get the all-important head nod that says, "Yeah, I get it," and avoid the, "I didn't know I couldn't wear my bedroom slippers to work," syndrome that comes with assuming they understand your policy. And before you leave this topic, ask all of your kidployees to sign an agreement stating they clearly understand what is acceptable and what is not.

If the language you use is unclear, kidployees will likely cut every corner they can. They'll leave one button undone, roll up their sleeves, and tilt their caps one way or the other simply to put their own unique spin on your dress code. Unless you accept this variation in your culture, take steps to avoid such leeway.

RESOLVING CONFLICT

You've laid down the law and they break it in ways like the following:

- Trevor shows up for work five minutes late for the second time this week.
- Courtney acts snotty toward a customer who's asking for change.
- Marcus didn't round up all the carts in the parking lot.

- Jerome and Katie are so busy talking about last night's concert, they're oblivious to the customers waiting to be served.
- Ashley is wearing her lip ring, even though she knows it's against the rules.

You want to scream, shout, or just send them home for the day. Yet you know it's your job to break through to them, correct their behavior, and put them back on track. Besides, if you send them home, they might not come back! So, are you supposed to expect this kind of behavior from your kidployees and occasionally look the other way?

No. But do fight the impulse to react in anger or respond dictatorially. Don't try to handle your front-liners the way your managers used to handle you, back when you were on the front line. Remember, they can't be managed the way you were. They're a different generation; getting the most from them requires a new set of tools.

When rules are broken in situations that don't call for immediate termination, gain your composure and think, "**O**pen **T**he **F**ront **D**oor **N**ow." OTFDN is the acronym for a terrific formula that helps you address—and correct—many nagging problems your kidployees create. Treating these problems according to the **O**pen **T**he **F**ront **D**oor **N**ow formula will get them back on your team.

Here's how the formula works.

O = Observe. First, make a statement about what you observe them doing (e.g., "Hey, Trevor, I saw that you arrived five minutes late on Tuesday and again today. . . ."). Notice that this statement isn't accusatory; you're simply making an observation. Pause briefly at this point to see if they inject a response. Maybe Trevor flatly denies being late, exposing a deeper problem you might have to contend with. Or maybe he gives you a piece of information you didn't know like, "Yes, but I told Mr. Martin last week that my mom would be out of town and I'd have to walk my brother home from school. He gave me the okay and said he'd let you know."

T = Thoughts. If your kidployees don't respond to your statements of observation, ask them for their thoughts on the matter (e.g., "So, what are your thoughts about treating customers a certain way, Courtney?"). This gives them a chance to show their cards and feel as though they're being heard. It also gives you an opportunity to find out if you need to know anything before you continue. It's critically important to allow them to make their case before moving forward.

F = Feedback. State the reasoning (the why) behind the rule that's been violated (e.g., "Marcus, when all the shopping carts aren't brought in at night, they often get stolen, vandalized, or damaged by cars that can't see them after the lights go off. Replacing and repairing carts cost a ton of money and affects how much we have left for employee raises . . . "). Give them feedback in a way that doesn't single out any one kidployee (e.g., Don't say: "Marcus, when *you* leave carts in the parking lot . . . "). Simply ask them to play by the same rules as everyone else for a good reason. Remember, your feedback becomes more effective when you tie it in to something that directly benefits them (like possibly getting a raise).

D = Desire. This step gives you the opportunity to state your desired expectation (e.g., "From this point on, Jerome and Katie, you're not allowed to carry on a conversation when customers are in your department. It's your job to engage with every shopper in your area to ensure people get the help they need."). Avoid making a statement from a point of weakness (e.g., "It would be really great if you could find another time . . . ") or one that's open to interpretation (e.g., "If it looks like a customer has a question, then please . . ."). Always be firm, concise, and extremely clear.

N = Next time. Without sounding as though you're issuing a threat, put in place a consequence for an undesired behavior if it's repeated (e.g., "If you're seen again with your lip ring in, Ashley, you'll be sent home and put on suspension for five days."). Also, avoid saying phrases like, "If I see you . . . ," and, "If I catch you . . . ," because they can turn you into the "bad cop" they watch out for. Avoid generalities like, "If that happens again, heads are going to roll!" and unreasonable consequences that you can't back up like, "If I see you with that lip ring in again, I'm going to pull it out of your face right then and there!" Instead, link each incorrect behavior to a specific consequence that's consistent, enforceable, and applicable to all front-liners regardless of age.

When you have to discipline your kidployees, make every effort to do so in private; they're extremely sensitive to embarrassment. A simple situation can escalate into an ugly mess by backing them into a corner while their peers watch. If you feel angry in the moment, walk away and compose yourself; you'll make better decisions after you've cooled down. Be sure to keep good notes and refer to them often to remind yourself about what works and what doesn't.

This formula is effective *only* if you use it in sequence. You can't follow just a few of these steps and expect the results you want. The more practice you get with this process, the more natural it will become for you. So think **O**pen **T**he **F**ront **D**oor **N**ow, and you'll find that "keeping the law" and "keeping your cool" go hand in hand.

15

HONESTY: IT'S THE BEST POLICY. WHAT'S YOURS?

Log onto the Internet, go to Google, enter the keywords *employee theft,* and you'll find *1.6 million* links. To say that this is a problem for your business—regardless of the business you're in—would be the understatement of the year. Take a look at the ugly statistics gleaned from a variety of business studies:

- Employee theft costs small business in America more than $40 billion each year. Total losses for large and small business exceed $200 billion annually.
- The retail industry lost $15.1 billion from employee theft in 2002. The food service industry lost almost $6 billion.
- The U.S. Chamber of Commerce reports that an employee is 15 times more likely to steal from an employer than a nonemployee. Unfortunately, 75 percent of employee-related crimes go unnoticed.
- Less than 10 percent of the employee population is responsible for more than 95 percent of the total losses from employee theft.
- Nearly every business experiences some degree of theft by employees.
- Nearly one-third of all bankruptcies are caused by employee theft.

You've been a victim. I've been a victim. And anyone who doesn't believe they've ever been a victim has also been a victim. It hits us in our wallets, and it hurts us in our hearts. We'd like to think that the people we accept into our families as employees would never, ever steal from us. When they do, it feels like a kick in the teeth.

As a freshman athlete in college, I was housed in an all-male dorm. Each night before bed, about 30 of us would walk to the taco joint next door and have a second dinner "on the house." The two high school girls running the night shift were more enamored with playing up to the college guys than keeping their boss in business. Ideally, I'd like to report that I never took advantage of the free food, and the restaurant manager discovered the theft and fired the two girls before the place went out of business—but neither statement would be true.

A year ago, my accountant tipped me off that several large deposits recorded for the previous year didn't add up. We began to call clients to trace invoices and payments received, and when the dust had settled, it became obvious that my administrative assistant had embezzled more than $15,000 from my business. Although I was extremely upset, the image that kept reappearing in my head was a pile of wadded-up burrito wrappers in my dorm room closet. I quickly realized two things:

1. Kids aren't the only ones who steal from an employer. (My assistant was a 43-year-old, married mother of three.)
2. In life, you reap what you sow.

Not Exclusive to Kids

Employee theft can take many forms, from stealing office supplies or merchandise, to stealing time by improperly reporting sick leave or by punching the time clock for another employee, to stealing intellectual property and confidential information. It isn't exclusive to any certain group or type of person, as employee theft crosses all boundaries of age, race, gender, and creed.

However, because of the inexperience, immaturity, and feeling of invincibility that accompany adolescence, kidployees are likely to be the biggest offenders of company theft—if not in actual dollar volume, then in frequency. Most experienced employers say off the cuff, "Young employees will steal you blind."

By nature, kids push the boundaries and test limits. As soon as you hire a kidployee, a friend catches wind of it quickly and asks, "Can you hook me up?" I wish I had the silver bullet that would completely eliminate employee theft from your workplace, but I don't. If you hire employees, you're vulnerable. If you hire kidployees, you've even more vulnerable.

No employer is 100-percent safe from employee theft and dishonesty. But you can put safeguards in place to keep the honest ones honest and root out those that aren't:

- Screen all job applicants.
- Tighten your security systems.
- Clearly spell out the rules.
- Eliminate temptation.
- Reach out and treat them fairly.
- Be the example.

SCREEN ALL JOB APPLICANTS

Unfortunately, some of your applicants have theft in mind from the start. You should be able to weed out these people by performing thorough background checks on all candidates. Thanks to technology and the wealth of providers available, a check can be done quickly and inexpensively, usually for less than $100.

Many applicants as young as 16 already have a job history. Don't hesitate to call previous employers to verify résumé and application information. Invest sufficient time to make sure applicants don't have a history of stealing from previous employers and that all credentials and references are valid. If a kid stretches the truth on an application, odds are that they can't be trusted as an employee.

Don't trust your gut feeling. Instead, establish a relationship with an agency that specializes in screening employees. Although their results won't be perfect, you stand a much better chance of knowing the kind of person you're hiring when you screen rather than if you just size them up for yourself. It's important, however, to have a bulletproof permission clause in your job application that's signed by both the applicant and a legal guardian, if necessary. Potential problem kidployees and overzealous parents could be looking for reasons to file a lawsuit.

TIGHTEN YOUR SECURITY SYSTEMS

For more than 30 years, *Mad* magazine featured "Spy vs. Spy," a cartoon strip in which two black-and-white, long-nosed characters were out to get each other. Each episode, one of the characters plotted to foil the other by using a new secret weapon. Comedy occurred as the plot backfired on the perpetrator, when the intended victim anticipated the attack and countered with an even cooler weapon.

That's the exact nature of store security. Every time a new employee theft security measure is created, a devious mind finds a way around it. Then a new security measure is activated to protect against that type of theft, and an employee finds a way to exploit that weakness. And on and on.

The cycle never ends, so you can never afford to stand pat and believe your business is theft proof. Always check your security measures for possible vulnerabilities and stay abreast of the latest employee theft protection technologies—as well as innovative ideas to protect you from devious minds.

Alarm Systems

Frequent and unannounced inventory inspections help keep dishonest kidployees off guard. Installing physical antitheft devices such as alarm systems and video surveillance cameras is costly but does serve as a deterrent. Be aware, however, that obvious measures can have a negative effect on morale. While overt tactics to deter theft help prevent losses, they also convey to kidployees that they can't be trusted.

CLEARLY SPELL OUT THE RULES

At 14, I was fishing off a concrete wall at a mountain reservoir, when a game warden approached me and handed me a ticket for illegal fishing. "Didn't you see the sign?" he asked.

"Sure, it says, 'No fishing off bridge or dyke.' That's why I came to this long piece of concrete," I replied.

"This *is* the dyke," the warden said.

"I didn't know this was considered a dyke!" I pleaded.

As he handed me the $20 fine, he made a statement I never forgot: "Ignorance is no excuse for breaking the law."

"I didn't know we weren't allowed to do that." What a common response when employees get caught breaking a company policy! Hearing that puts you in the situation of playing Judge Judy and deciding if an incident was based on ignorance or intent. That's not a position you want to be in. And that's why it's critical to eliminate this, "I didn't know . . ." reply from their vocabularies.

Handling Cash Rules

Clearly spelling out the rules for handling cash and merchandise early in the training process is essential. Don't leave any rule open to interpretation. Are they allowed to take samples? Can their friends also get an employee discount? Can they carry the night deposit home and take it to the bank the next day if they sense they're being followed by thugs?

Be 100 percent crystal clear about conveying your rules in plain, simple language. Make sure every employee reads those rules and signs off on them. Then be certain that you also clearly define and enforce the consequences for anyone who disobeys them.

ELIMINATE TEMPTATION

As much as you'd like *not* to believe it, everyone has a breaking point, even an Opie. In the ebb and flow of life, every one of your kidployees will be found in a cash pinch, needing money to bail them out of a jam, make rent, pay tuition, help a friend, and more. If that situation intersects with a moment of unsupervised cash or merchandise handling, the temptation could prove overwhelming. Therefore, the best prevention strategy is to eliminate tempting opportunities.

Handling Cash Two-Step

For example, always make handling daily cash receipts a two-step process. Have one person take the totals from cash registers and balance back to the person handling the money. Shifting responsibilities from one person to another allows them to check each other's work for accuracy and suspicious activities. Establish a system of checks and balances for key processes, ensuring that different people perform various tasks and routinely review each other's work. This also makes collusion between employees, or between an employee and an outside source, difficult. Tell all employees that, by doing this, you'll significantly reduce this type of theft.

Another familiar technique for skimming cash from the daily take is to ring up a sale, void it, and pocket the cash. That's why cash registers display signs asking customers to make certain they get a receipt—and even go as far as stating, "Failure to give you a receipt means your meal is free."

Giveaways to Friends

A frequently used method of employee theft is giving away merchandise or food to friends (like the girls at the taco joint during my college years). Some managers set policies that prohibit employees from processing transactions with friends and family, although this can be difficult to administer.

Your procedures can go a long way toward reducing temptation. Lessons learned from past experiences—both yours and others in your line of work—can help you establish those procedures and make stealing more difficult.

REACH OUT AND TREAT THEM FAIRLY

"They owed me."

After getting nailed for theft and being asked, "Why'd you do it?" that's the most common response a kidployee will give.

If young workers believe they're getting a raw deal (such as not earning fair and equitable pay, not getting credit for hours worked, or feeling overworked and underappreciated), they might try to extract revenge— or even the score—by stacking some of your chips onto their plate. You'd like to think that a disgruntled kidployee would approach you to work out the problem, and many do. But a lack of maturity and experience leave many teenage front-liners not knowing how to talk with managers or properly express a greivance. I know that, at 15, I certainly didn't know how to approach Mr. Wong with my concerns.

This goes back to being as fair, open, and humane as you can to your young staffers. Keeping the communication lines open lets you head off minor problems before they become big ones. If your kidployee gets so upset with you or your company that they'd steal from you, and you don't know it, then security isn't your real problem—it's poor communication.

Expressing Problems

Wise managers make it easy for kidployees to express problems and concerns. For example, a small chain of quick-service restaurants in Denver surveys its kidployees each month and invites kids to share anything bothering them in an open note to the owner. This way, if a kid feels wronged or taken advantage of by the store manager, they have a chance to be heard at a higher level. Further, if they know about a coworker who dips into the till, they can alert management anonymously without fear of retribution.

It only makes sense to strive toward developing a healthy relationship with your kidployees. Get to know them on a personal level. (See the ideas discussed in Chapter 17.) Generally, even a kid who's predisposed to theft won't steal from you if they like you, believe that you like them, and feels that you've always treated them fairly. It's simply tough to steal from someone you care about.

Lastly, do everything you can to compensate your kidployees well. Paying them above the going rate and having an attractive recognition and rewards program helps make them value the job all the more. It also serves as a great reminder that they can't go just anywhere and find a good job like this. You'll see that doing this will eliminate the "they owe me" feeling before it starts.

BE THE EXAMPLE

My son landed his first-ever job in the sporting goods department of a large national retailer. He was paid an hourly wage plus a percentage override for sales generated each day. He also received an incentive for selling extended service agreements on large-ticket items. All employees were given a quota for selling these agreements, because the practice provided a high-profit revenue stream for the retailer.

Unknown to many consumers, a significant percentage of products in the store were already covered by a manufacturer's warranty that was more than adequate. Extended warranties aren't always a rip-off, but occasionally scare tactics and unlikely scenarios are used to boost their sales.

Every Saturday morning before the store opened, the general manager (GM) held a store meeting with mandatory attendance. As employees walked into the meeting, the song "Money, Money, Money" by the Ojays (the theme song used in NBC's reality show *The Apprentice*) blared over the sound system. Then, in a highly charged meeting, the GM gave a fire-and-brimstone pump-up talk to the salespeople, many of whom were under 18. In rah-rah fashion, he'd encourage all salespeople to push the extended service agreements with every big-ticket item sold. But he never gave any instructions on how to determine whether a customer needed extended service or any examples of how service agreements had helped previous customers. The sole instruction was: "Sell these agreements, or we'll find someone else who will."

As the meeting concluded—and just before he unlocked the doors for customers to enter the store—he smiled and turned his staff loose by saying, "Let's leave 'em broke in the aisles!" They understood that this left-handed innuendo meant, "Let's make as much money from the people who enter the store as we can." By implication, he was also saying, "There will be winners and losers here today, and we want to be on the winning side."

According to my son, the store had a high turnover rate, and employee theft ran rampant. The general manager never realized that his admonition to make as much money as possible at the customers' expense completely turned off his kidployees who, in their short lives, had already seen a world of people being "taken." Some (like my son) quit, while others stole. But certainly the manager's ethics influenced his kidployees. (He has since been replaced and the store is faring much better.)

Taking Advantage

Companies whose systems take advantage of customers sooner or later realize that ethical lapses return to haunt them. Their kidployees are the first to surreptitiously rebel, thinking, "If my boss will lie to customers to make more money, my boss will also lie to me." In this scenario, why would kidployees ever give a damn?

> Emphasize how customers benefit, and let your kidployees know that, by pointing them toward better values, everyone comes out on top. The customer gets more for the dollars spent, the company increases its profits, and the kidployee gets a perk for making it happen—a win-win-win situation. They will see upselling as an honest, value-added proposition and not a scam.

Profit isn't a dirty word to kidployees who want to help your business make money. But don't think you can get them to upsell simply to line your company's pockets, even if they make more money themselves in the process.

Cooking the Books

Your kidployees have been bombarded with messages of dishonesty. Headlines are filled with stories ranging from corporations that have "cooked the books" to athletes who have "corked the bats." It's no longer a matter of what you do; it's what the authorities can prove. There's a difference between being *innocent* and being found *not guilty*.

Remember, your employees' eyes are upon you. You can't allow yourself—or anyone in your company—to perpetuate a message (or an example) of anything that's not 100-percent ethical and above board. You can't be "kind of honest," just like a woman can't be "kind of pregnant." Always model the highest standards of honesty, character, and integrity with customers, vendors, employees, your up-line managers and executives, and/or stockholders.

Your front-liners won't follow your words and be intimidated by your threats. They will, however, follow your example—even when you don't think they're watching.

16

MENTORSHIP: SIMON SAYS, "LEAD THE WAY"

Although Simon Says is a game for children, it's been used in business meetings to get an audience involved. In this game, everyone stands and follows Simon's commands, trying hard to ignore what Simon is actually doing. Those who mimic Simon's actions instead of his verbal commands—or even hesitate slightly—must take a seat. When an experienced Simon leads the exercise, it takes only minutes before the entire audience is seated. Why? Because it's nearly impossible to do only what Simon *says;* the overwhelming compulsion is to do what Simon *does.*

Your front-liners play Simon Says 24/7, and, like or not, you are Simon. You can't say one thing and do another, then expect them to do what you said. They will follow your example. While this is true of leadership in general, it's particularly true when leading today's 16- to 24-year-old employees.

While most people in business—regardless of their level—experience constant transition (always anticipating a bigger, better deal), today's kidployees are looking for a solid Simon that will be an ethical guide. But, being street-smart and wise beyond their years, they won't orient their moral compass on just anyone with a fancy title and a corner office. To win the hearts and minds of this new generation takes a "do as I do" Simon. Four core characteristics of effective Simons are the following:

1. Impassioned people of character
2. Always looking for connecting points
3. Powerful communicators
4. Ever-mindful of their actions

EFFECTIVE SIMONS ARE IMPASSIONED PEOPLE OF CHARACTER

Try the following experiment, completing all three steps before reading further:

1. Using either the margin on this page or a blank piece of a paper, write down the names of five people who have been the biggest positive influences in your life. List people you have known personally.
2. Next, cross out the name(s) of those on your list you believe possess(ed) weak character or lack(ed) high moral integrity.
3. Finally, go back over your list and cross out the name(s) of those you believe lacked—to any degree—passion and/or emotion for their careers, beliefs, and hobbies.

If you're like most, your list will be comprised almost exclusively of people who came into your life before age 21. It likely includes a teacher, coach, parent or other relative, religious leader, and/or maybe even one of your first bosses. Regardless of who's made the list, I bet a dollar to a dime's worth of donuts that you crossed out none of their names.

People have always been drawn to impassioned Simons of character. These Simons didn't need to have a formal title that indicated they were in charge (e.g., manager, principal, CEO, etc.). You wanted to follow their lead because they had a fire burning in their bellies for what they believed in. What they did was so hot that when you stood close to them, you felt the heat. You could trust them because they were honest, straight shooters. You never worried that they'd pull a fast one or manipulate you for their own gain. And when they told you something, you could hang your hat on it.

Although Simon Says is a game built around a leader purposefully trying to mislead you, an effective Simon in the real world never will. As the previous chapter pointed out, in today's world, people of uncompromising character are an endangered species. That's why kidployees naturally gravitate toward solid Simons; when they encounter one, they want to stay close.

Being Impassioned

Consider this. The basic aim of this book is how to get your kidployees to give a damn about your business. That assumes, of course, that you give a damn yourself. Your passion for what you do, or lack thereof, bleeds through in every word you say and every action you take. Trying to get buy in from them when you haven't fully bought in yourself is like trying to return from a place you've never been.

> Here's the bonus: Impassioned managers seldom have to post job openings. When word spreads that they're hiring, every available applicant within earshot lines up to become the next apprentice.

No matter how good your acting skills, if you don't believe in what you're doing or for whom you're doing it, you won't be able to convince your front-liners that you're for real—at least not for long. They need to see, hear, and feel your passion and your commitment before they jump in and let go. They want to know that you firmly believe in the company's products or services before being asked to represent them to the buying public.

Effective Simons in the workplace feel impassioned about their company and their industry. They live and breathe their business and radiate their passion, enticing those who surround them to believe there's no better job in the world. They don't complain about the current state of affairs or whine when things go awry. Instead, they exude hope and confidence.

ALWAYS LOOKING FOR CONNECTING POINTS

Harvey McKay is the founder and CEO of the McKay Envelope Company. An acclaimed keynote speaker, he's also the author of numerous *New York Times* bestseller business books, including *Swim with the Sharks*. In this book, MacKay revealed his secret to building an $85 million-per-year envelope company—a questionnaire he developed in the early years called The MacKay 66.

MacKay instructed his salespeople to use this questionnaire to find out 66 pieces of information about each prospect and customer. But he didn't seek information about buying cycles or budgets for envelopes. The MacKay 66 encouraged his salespeople to discover personal things about the person buying the envelopes through casual conversation and observation. For example, the salesperson would ask, "Where did you go to college? What's your favorite restaurant? What are your career goals?

What are the names of your children?" MacKay knew that in gaining insights about each prospect, each salesperson would undoubtedly find
commonalities that could become the nucleus of a friendship (e.g., "Hey,
I play tournament croquet, too!"). Given a choice, people prefer to do
business with friends.

Get to Know Them

In today's fast-paced business environment, most managers simply
don't take time to get to know any more about their kidployees than
what's written on their job applications, if even that. Instead, they think,
"There's work to do here, so let's dispense with the nicey-nice and get to
it." Even when such managers don't know anything about their staffers
beyond their job qualifications, they somehow believe they can get their
front-liners to buy in to the job. As we learned from the "Pagoda principle" in Chapter 1, this doesn't happen.

Effective Simons have their own version of the MacKay 66. They invest time (and it's truly an investment) to learn all they can about their
recruits, then build on those connection points (e.g., "So you went fishing this weekend, huh? Me too! We'll have to schedule a time to go together."). They ask a lot of questions, take a lot of notes, and create a file
for each young staffer to remind them about hobbies, interests, family
members, and so on. They creatively acknowledge birthdays, gradua-
tions, and special events. Knowing the hopes and aspirations of each kidployee, when they come across an article that would interest them, they
clip it and hand it to them. Effective Simons let their actions say, "I know
who you are and what matters to you, and I support you fully."

Compound Interest

Buy in is the compound interest you receive on the principal you
deposit; the more you put in, the more you get out. How many points
would your cashier move up on the GAD scale if you offered to donate
the refreshments for their church choir's fundraiser? Imagine the long-
range impact you'd have on a kidployee if you cheered them on at her
tennis match. What added emotion would your busboy bring to the job
Monday if they saw your face at their band's concert Saturday night?

An old adage says, "People don't care how much you know, until they
know how much you care." You can be absolutely brilliant when it comes
to the workings of your business, but if you don't care enough about

your front-line employees to search for—and exploit—connecting points, they will certainly care less about you and your business.

EFFECTIVE SIMONS ARE POWERFUL COMMUNICATORS

You just wrote down the names of five people who are/were positive influences in your life. The first person to complete this exercise was me. Before sending this chapter off to my editor, I took out a pen and wrote down the five most influential positive people I've ever encountered. As I reviewed my list and looked for common denominators, I realized that all five were people I had met before I turned 20. Each was an impassioned person of character and, importantly, a powerful communicator.

As a professional speaker, I can speak with confidence in front of almost any audience. However, none of the five influencers on my list ever earned a cent giving a speech—and I doubt any of them ever held a microphone for more than a minute or two. But all of them knew how to get inside my head and my heart, deliver their unique message, and bring out the best in me.

Speak Their Language

No matter what message you want to send to your front-liners, know how to get inside their heads and their hearts to elicit a favorable response. This requires that you not only establish connecting points but that you communicate in terms they understand. Kidployees have their own language, and even though you shouldn't attempt to speak hip hop or street lingo with them—you'll sound silly—it's important that you understand the world they live in.

The use of Internet chat rooms and tightly targeted television programs on networks such as MTV, the WB, and UPN provide an instant exchange of dialog and fashion: what's cool one minute is "so yesterday" the next. The use of phrases, gestures, and body language evolves at a frightening pace. To have any hope of connecting with your kidployees, it's best to keep dialed in to the same frequency they are.

Effective Simons are powerful communicators, because they listen to the people they lead, thereby understanding their internal motivators. Before conveying a point, they make sure they've broken through the intended recipient's preoccupation so they can address a captive audience. Then, with the precision of a surgeon, they impart their message—and expected outcomes—in clear, easy-to-understand terms. When they finish—instead of assuming their message was understood—they elicit feedback to make absolutely certain what was said was also what was heard.

EFFECTIVE SIMONS ARE EVER-MINDFUL OF THEIR ACTIONS

At age six, my son asked me why I had two garage door openers on my sun visor. When I told him only one of them was a garage door opener, he asked what the other one was. Without thinking, I blurted out, "It's a radar detector." His reply almost sent me through the windshield. "You have that so the mean police don't catch you speeding?" When we got home, I threw that second "garage door opener" in the trash and realized I couldn't ever switch off being a father.

Effective Simons know that they always have to be switched on, because they're being watched and emulated all the time. Ever mindful of their actions, they uphold the highest standards of honesty and integrity, play by the rules, and present themselves as consummate professionals. Most of all, they serve as consistent models for what they want their frontline workforce to be.

Whenever I'm in a restaurant, a mass retail store, or a supermarket during a hectic rush, I always scan the floor to see if I can spot the general manager. Over the years, I have found an amazing overlap between businesses that ran smoothly and those in which the head honcho worked on the floor wiping tables, bagging groceries, waiting on customers, etc. While keeping an eye on their troops to make certain they get support, these leaders demonstrate an all-hands-on-deck approach as if to say, "We're all in this together!" It's at these crucial moments young people learn to perform under pressure; they emulate what they see.

Brother Leo

An old legend tells of a monastery in France that was well known throughout Europe because of the extraordinary leadership of a man known only as Brother Leo. To learn from him, several monks began a pilgrimage to visit Brother Leo. Almost immediately, the monks began to bicker over who should do various chores. On the third day, they met another monk who was also going to the monastery, and he joined their troupe. This monk never complained or shirked a duty; whenever the others fought over a chore, he would gracefully volunteer and simply do it himself.

By the last day, the other monks were following his example and worked together smoothly. When they finally reached the monastery and asked for Brother Leo, they discovered it was Brother Leo who had joined them on his way back to the monastery. Through his actions, he had showed them the way.

Effective Simons aren't the kind of managers who walk around barking orders at the grunts; rather, they're like Brother Leo. Kidployees see them grab the mop to clean the floor and learn how the floor should be mopped. They see how their manager diffuses a snobby customer with warmth, compassion, and a smile, and they discover how to win over difficult people. They're never put in a compromising situation or asked to cover up for their manager's mistake. They're never required to fib to a caller that, "The manager's not in right now," because their leaders always model responsibility and straightforwardness. Through the ever-mindful actions of these Simons, kidployees internalize their own definitions of ethics, punctuality, and professional appearance. Even away from the workplace, effective Simons are "on" as they embody the highest standards.

LINKING EFFECTIVE SIMONS TO YOUR FRONT LINE

An organization can be chock-full of Simons and still fail miserably when it comes to leading its front-line staff. Somewhere between the CEO and the kid at the cash register, the trickle-down theory of leadership stops trickling. The visions, goals, objectives, purposes, and missions that become established in the boardroom don't filter down the organization chart to the front-line masses. No matter how great the game plan is, if it can't be executed in the trenches, mediocrity abounds.

Freshman-Senior Link

In the early '90s, when I gave presentations almost exclusively to high school students, a youth speaker colleague and friend, Phil Boyte, envisioned a solution for an epidemic spreading throughout public education. With the drop-out rate for high school freshmen soaring alarmingly, Phil thought, "The reason so many freshman are dropping out is because no one notices them dropping in." He then created a program, called Link Crew®, designed to link every incoming freshman with a senior mentor at the school. The idea was simple yet profound. Instead of getting hazed by seniors, freshmen would be warmly welcomed by an upperclassman who would tour them around campus, introduce them to other people, and make certain they felt comfortable. Through this initiative, each freshman links to an experienced, mature student whom they can ask for help and friendly advice. As you might imagine, Phil's program has grown in leaps and bounds. It's now in thousands of schools throughout North America.

Although mentoring is nothing new in corporate America, it's extremely rare on the front lines of businesses, particularly in the service sector. While turnover continues to wreak havoc and customer service is pathetic, business leaders might be overlooking a simple solution to their dilemma—linking each kidployee to an effective Simon or, if a Simon isn't available, at least an Opie in the workplace.

Linking in Action

A number of leading-edge companies have put this principle into practice and experienced great success. Consider these examples:

- At W.L. Gore & Associates, the maker of Goretex®, new hires are assigned a sponsor, an associate who helps the newcomer become rapidly acclimated and productive. A key goal is to find a "quick win"—a project or idea that puts the person on a fast track to accomplishment and to new projects and responsibilities. Sponsors give the person a basic understanding of his or her commitments and what it takes to succeed in those commitments. Helping others achieve success is a key criterion for all Gore associates.
- SEI Investments, a leading global provider of asset management and investment technology solutions, has a stellar record of motivating and retaining its young workers. The company understands their kidployees' deep need for learning, so it organizes staff in teams to allow frequent changes of job assignment and crosslearning. The company doesn't hesitate to let young team members take on new challenges. It also encourages them to take advantage of the company's mentor network for guidance as well as to identify opportunities for education and new job assignments.
- General Electric went a step further when it developed the concept of reverse mentoring. This concept encourages managers to

dip into the ranks to find a tech-savvy employee to coach them on how to improve their computer and online skills. GE discovered that bonds between upper managers and front-liners form more quickly when each party brings something of value to the equation.

Link to a Solid Subordinate

If your front-liners are not yet linked at least to a solid fellow employee, they need to be. Invest the time to develop a good mentoring program, and you'll find that your linked kidployees are much more likely to buy in to your business and stay on your payroll. What's more, you'll find training them and communicate with them easier. Not only will their performance and productivity improve, but the service they provide your customers will be better than that of nonlinked kidployees.

17

SERVICE: KEEPING YOUR YOUNGEST EMPLOYEES FROM DRIVING AWAY YOUR OLDEST CUSTOMERS

Being on the receiving end of really bad customer service is no longer something you rush to tell your friends and family about. Twenty years ago, these incidents were as rare as alien sightings. Now they're so commonplace, people experience them every day, and yours have become nothing special. In fact, you could fill a book with your own personal horror stories, and you wouldn't just be referring to the unacceptable service you received from kidployees. Really bad service runs rampant; a service provider's age is no predictor of service quality.

No wonder companies are fazing people out of front-line customer contact positions. In today's world, consumers routinely make purchases at the supermarket, process complex banking transactions, pay highway tolls, book airline travel, and rent home movies without human contact. Why should people help us do these things any more? RoboStaff is on the job.

With user-friendly touch screens, voice recognition technology, and magnetic strip readers, sophisticated RoboStaffers have invaded the point-of-purchase arena—and they're multiplying in droves. Like vending machines on steroids, they authorize us to fill up our gas tanks, hand us our boarding passes, and ring up our nuts and bolts at Home Depot. Even McDonald's, once renowned for friendly service by well-trained teenage employees, now has restaurants where customers place and pay for their own orders through RoboStaff. Simply swipe your credit card, and your chip-enhanced buddy takes it from there.

From a manager's perspective, RoboStaffers could solve many of the nightmarish personnel problems you face. You don't have to worry about machines calling in sick or showing up out of uniform. They won't ask for a raise, they won't steal from you, and they'll never be rude or disrespectful to you or your customers. Still, having RoboStaffers on your front line creates an enormous gap between your products and your consumers— an automatic disconnect.

Futurists were wrong when, a decade ago, they prognosticated that technology would soon supplant the need for people on our front lines. Studies continue to prove that, although consumers might shop for products and compare prices online, they demand personal attention before, during, and after the sale. In fact, they'll go out of their way and pay more to get it.

> Like you, given a choice between transacting business with a competent, knowledgeable, friendly kidployee or a RoboStaffer, your customers will pick the one with a heartbeat every time. But if your front-liners fail to be competent, knowledgeable, and friendly, an automaton on your competitor's front line will take their orders without thinking twice.

The bad news? Customer service in America has become cold, lifeless, and robotic. The good news? If you can train your front line to consistently deliver top-quality service that's even better than what a RoboStaffer delivers, you'll win the business nine out of ten times. More than that, price will cease to be the primary differentiator between you and your competitors.

FIVE KEYS FOR TRAINING

How do you train your kidployees to deliver outstanding service, thereby preventing your youngest employees from driving away your oldest customers? The five keys are the following:

1. Open their eyes.
2. Coach like a coach.
3. Empower your kidployees to serve.
4. Reward service excellence.
5. Model, mentor, and motivate.

OPEN THEIR EYES

A child who's grown up in the Amazon jungles and has never seen a saxophone player can't dream of being a saxophone player. The child hasn't heard the sound of a saxophone, has no idea that one exists, and wouldn't know what one looked like if he stumbled across it. So, show the kid a saxophone . . .

As the adage goes, you can't give away what you've never had. The 16- to 24-year-old kidployees standing between you and your customers have transacted business more times with RoboStaffers than with humans. They don't remember the "service with a smile" and "the customer is king" era of days gone by. They've likely never experienced good service as a consumer—so how can they deliver it as your front-line employees?

Answer: They can't. However, if you took them out of the jungle, exposed them to the saxophone, and let them hear the sweet sound of impeccable service—well, then they'd have a frame of reference.

Field Trip #1: Take Them to Nordstrom

Consider taking your front-line kidployees on a field trip to a Nordstrom (or another acclaimed customer-centered retailer) and allow them to observe legendary customer service firsthand. Show them the difference between someone who just works at a job and a career professional who delights customers with every contact.

How can taking a trip to a fine restaurant or full-service retailer be an illuminating experience for your new recruits? They'll see how top-quality merchants feature staff who dress professionally, smile gregariously to everyone they meet, show expertise in product knowledge, give customers their complete and undivided attention, and go out of their way to please their customers—even those who are not spending a lot of money. Take them down the aisles to where packages are wrapped and bagged. Have them take mental notes about everything they see. Then, on the way back to your store, ask them to state their observations and list ways they can improve their own delivery of service.

Field Trip #2: Show Them Service That's Horrific

Your front-liners can learn as much from observing what *not* to do as they can from experiencing excellence. The impact increases when they're required to compare the two extremes from a customer's perspective.

Recently, I chose to take a low-fare airline from Denver to Tampa. I proceeded to the counter where Amber, a young counter agent, checked me in for my flight. Based on the quality of service she provided, I thought she was much older than she actually was. After all, isn't customer service a skill developed over time? Shouldn't the best providers of service naturally be the oldest and most experienced?

Although she appeared young, Amber was incredibly competent at her job as she helped me make several last-minute, complex changes to my itinerary. She was also one of the warmest and friendliest airline employees I'd ever encountered. No request of mine seemed to rattle her. Even though long waiting lines were bursting with anxious holiday travelers, her delightful and charming demeanor was constant. The other agents for this airline seemed to share Amber's zeal, appearing happy and eager to serve.

Surprised by this strange phenomenon, I investigated further. Drawing on my vast experience, laser wit, and keen mind, I hit Amber with an intense question designed to reveal the mystery of her upbeat attitude and expertise. "Amber," I pried with the intensity of Johnny Cochran, "Why are you so dang cheerful and helpful today?"

"It's simple," she answered. "As a part of our training, the company makes us visit the counters of the big three air carriers and watch their agents for an hour or two. It's easy to see how miserable most of them are and how they pass on their misery to their customers. Then they make us promise we'll never, ever become like those guys."

I walked away enlightened like a monk in an orchard. It's not only about training people to do the right things; it's about showing them the result of doing the wrong things.

The Good, the Bad, and the Ugly

Customers today experience three levels of service: Nordstrom's, Service that's Ugly, and indifferent. Most experiences fall into the third category—that is, when the transaction is complete, the customer feels neither special nor angry. If getting that result is your goal, then look into replacing your front-liners with RoboStaff. However, if delivering excellent service is something you strive for, make certain that your front-liners know what excellence looks like and feels like.

COACH LIKE A COACH

Any football coach preparing his team for a game knows the importance of practice. To have any chance of victory, his players must be ready to meet their opponents and be fully prepared to react in any situation. Like a football team, your front-liners must be prepared to meet any challenge customers throw at them. You can simply manage them, but if you want to win on the service playing field, do more than just manage. Coach like a coach.

Lay Out a Winning Game Plan

Of course, you know *why* you want your customers treated well and *how* that will pay off for you and your business, but don't assume your front-liners know, too. If you want them on your team working toward the goals you set, they need to understand those goals and know how they will pay off for you and your business. More importantly, they need to know how customer service will pay off for them.

As street-smart as your front-liners are, they might not truly comprehend two things: that happy customers come back and that really happy customers tell their friends. A good coach makes absolutely certain their kidployees understand the direct connection between happy customers and increased hours, wages, and benefits for those on the front line.

Practice, Practice, Practice

Every successful coach knows that, "The way you practice is the way you play." Equating this principle to your role as the service coach means your job is never finished. How do you get your front-liners to deliver the service you want them to deliver consistently? By consistently working with them. It's not like showing them how to balance a cash drawer or take out the garbage one time. You can't demonstrate service once and feel confident that they've got it. Instead, prepare them for almost anything, so they're never caught off guard by something that happens in a customer interaction.

Start by role-playing almost every possible scenario. Doing practice situations, have kidployees take turns alternating between the role of the customer and the front-liner. Focus each session on a common scenario in your particular business and introduce various types of customers they might encounter. This way, they can observe how to creatively solve problems for customers without breaking store policies and know how to diffuse tense situations while making customers feel valued.

> Practicing through role-playing keeps your staff learning, growing, and focusing on customer service.

Have your kidployees set up role-playing using a scenario they recently encountered, either in their own experience or a situation they observed. Allow them to assume the character of the customer, rotating in different front-liners to see how each would or should respond. Also demonstrate the desired behavior, then invite kidployees to evaluate the techniques they saw. Ask each person how the interaction could be improved. Keep all conversations focused on solutions, not on critiquing the actors. Conclude each practice role-play with clearly stated steps for handling customers in those situations.

Pump 'Em Up

Nothing can rally your front-liners like a call to glory from their team coach. As long as your pregame speeches aren't overemotional or given too frequently, a well-thought-out, short speech can ignite their spirit of service. Remember to emphasize the team concept, articulate your expectations, and convince them that providing great service is in their best interest.

Restaurant managers often huddle team members together for a few minutes before the doors open to explain chef specials, point out areas for team improvement, make announcements, and align the front-of-the-house employees with those working behind the scenes. Many retailers also hold preshift meetings to discuss inventory changes and bring attention to key areas for improvement. Most importantly, a huddle gives a manager the platform to praise top performers publicly, reveal new developments, and encourage the entire staff to work cooperatively to make certain all customers receive the ultimate in service.

Wide Inclusion

It's important to coach *all* of your kidployees about delivering great service, not just those who actually interface with your customers. Your business could encounter an unexpected rush, forcing you to pull people from your loading dock or kitchen to work with customers, or they could be promoted to a customer contact position. But even if they don't directly interact with your customers, they do interact with vendors, each other, and you. Service training will only improve their interpersonal communication skills, thereby improving the quality and stability of your entire workforce.

EMPOWER YOUR KIDPLOYEES TO SERVE

If customers are unhappy with your products, services, or policies, they'll probably confront the first employee they see and demand satisfaction. Odds are, that first person is a front-line kidployee. If this happens, how will your kidployee respond?

Although front-liners are expected to deliver good service to happy customers, most are rendered powerless when it comes to dealing with a complaint. "I'll have to go find a manager to help you," is the typical response. Then the disgruntled customer is asked to wait until someone with the authority to handle the problem arrives on the scene. This not only further alienates the unhappy customer but sends a message to kids on the front lines that they are just grunts who can't be trusted to handle a tough situation on their own. As a manager, you won't have much luck getting buy in from an untrustworthy grunt.

So, are you expected to trust the decision-making ability of 16- or 17-year-old kids? What if they make a mistake and promise too much or do too little? How can you feel confident that your front-liners can effectively handle a customer complaint? As you'll discover in Chapter 21, training and trusting are key.

Putting on the Ritz

In the Ritz Carlton hotel chain, front-line employees are empowered to spend up to $1,000 to solve a customer problem. Although resolving an issue rarely takes anywhere close to that amount (most situations require less than $25), imagine the confidence that Ritz Carlson employees exude when faced with a challenge. Also, consider the effect on Ritz service if their front-liners did *not* have this power. If staffers had to seek approval for every nickel and dime expended to redress a legitimate beef, management would be up to its eyeballs in paperwork, and the Ritz Carlton would be just another hotel. In fact, empowering front-line staff to this degree hasn't cost the Ritz; it's strengthened its brand, made its operation more efficient, and reduced turnover.

Of course, it wouldn't make sense to empower pizza delivery drivers to spend up to $1,000 to remedy a grievance. They could, however, be empowered to comp a pizza or throw in some breadsticks to soothe an angry customer, thus making the cost relative to the service being rendered.

Empowering your front-liners means training them to respond in a variety of situations, coaching them with role-playing, and trusting them to make good decisions. Even though they'll make mistakes, you'll find that the advantages will eclipse the mistakes by far—as empowered kidployees register much higher on the GAD continuum than mere grunts.

REWARD SERVICE EXCELLENCE

In Chapter 10, I made a case for the "what gets rewarded gets repeated" theory. This especially rings true when you catch your front-liners giving great service. If you acknowledge their performance, point out what they did right, and reward them on the spot, that level of service happens again and again. In addition, other front-liners will witness (or catch wind of) the rewarded occurrence and make an effort to duplicate it. Great service begets great service.

For a few weeks during the summer of 1995, I played the role of "the Attitude Guy" for Elitch Gardens, the largest amusement park in the Rocky Mountain Region. The experiment gave me an open lab to see how on-the-spot reward programs affect customer service. Each day, I strolled through the park as a mystery guest. When I spotted kidployees going out of their way to make my (or any other guest's) park experience better, I approached them and introduced myself as "the Attitude Guy." Then I handed them a "pog" (the wooden nickel–type trading toy that was popular in the early 1990s) that they could exchange for a cool prize.

As word spread among the park's 1,800 kidployees about a strange "attitude guy" walking around handing out pogs to those employees who were delighting guests, complaints dropped, and guest satisfaction scores on comment cards rose 38 percent.

Always be prepared to reward great service as it happens—in the same way you're prepared to discipline a kidployee who's rude to a guest or ignores a customer wanting help. Be on the lookout for moments of excellence and be equally prepared to call attention to them.

Involve Your Customers

Guests staying at a Hilton property (Hampton Inn, Doubletree, Embassy Suites, etc.) might notice a stack of colorful *Catch Me at My Best!* comment cards on the front counter as they check in. These clever cards invite guests to write notes directly to the general manager. They're designed to capture guests' sentiments rather than having them check a series of boxes corresponding to a predetermined set of categories.

Hilton guests are asked to provide direct feedback on the service they receive from a particular employee by writing a brief note that begins, "Dear General Manager, I caught _____ at his/her best!" followed by a series of blank lines. A guest might choose to heap praise on a bellhop, a front desk attendant, a housekeeper, a gift shop employee, or the busboy who kept their juice glass filled.

You can imagine how hotel employees feel when managers call them out and tell them they were caught red-handed. Expecting discipline, the front-liner instead receives a high five and perhaps an award or a nifty perk instead. This can only stimulate others to go out of their way and get "caught and turned in" by a guest.

Whatever you do, make certain your front-line staff gets recognized and rewarded for providing exceptional service. Whatever the cost, you reap handsome returns on your investment plus happier customers and greater buy in from your staff.

MODEL, MENTOR, AND MOTIVATE

Like most people who shop online, I am paranoid about getting burned. That's why, before I push the button marked *Purchase* from any vendor, I always check reviews from past customers to see if they have been burned.

This practice transcends online shopping and certainly transcends my own personal habits. I've come to believe that, in a service-based economy, a business is only as good as its most recent customer says it is.

Unless your ultimate plan calls for abandoning great customer service in favor of the dependable mediocrity of RoboStaff, you can't rest on the customer service coaching you gave your front-liners today; you have to follow it up with another helping tomorrow. You'll find examples of good and bad service everywhere you look; in your experience—as well as in the experiences of your kidployees—much can be learned, refined, and perfected.

Continually reinforce the importance of outstanding customer service. To keep them focused on their most important responsibility, ask your kidployees questions like, "What did you do today to delight customers?" and, "What are the people you served today saying about us to their friends?" Give them the opportunity to respond at length about how they made a customer's day. Kidployees learn more from their direct supervisors than they ever will from the best video or training module. Every time a manager pulls them aside and praises them for something they did well or suggests ways they could have handled a situation better, their ability to interface with customers improves.

> Every occasion where kidployees can observe how their manager serves a guest provides a benchmark for how they should deliver service. But it's how a manager treats them directly that proves to be the single greatest factor for shaping how they themselves will provide service.

It's a chain reaction, to be sure. The way your kidployees treat your customers mirrors the way you treat them. You can't berate, embarrass, ridicule, or talk down to your front-liners and expect them to roll out the red carpet for your customers. It won't happen—not unless they know you're watching them with whip in hand. Conversely, if you're positive, upbeat, and always supportive of your front-liners, you'll see that attitude reflected in the gleaming eyes of your patrons.

The Challenge Ahead

Make no mistake, your front-liners can delight your customers and keep them coming back, or they can drive them away and into the awaiting arms of a RoboStaffed competitor. Given a choice, your customers prefer to do business with a competent person who has a kind heart, a willing spirit, and a smiling face.

Unfortunately, your emerging front-liners don't come prewired to these specifications, so you've got your work cut out for you. Turn to the five steps covered in this chapter; they provide a template for you to gain—and keep—the service advantage you want.

WHO'S GETTING IT RIGHT?

*How Forward-Thinking Organizations
Got Them to Give a Damn*

18

STONE COLD
CRAZY KIDPLOYEES

"**N**ow Auditioning!" This announcement might apply to a Broadway play or even an indie film. It's also a casting-call notice posted in the window of a friendly neighborhood ice cream store that wants to hire a few Opies.

Scottsdale, Arizona-based Cold Stone Creamery is the fastest growing ice cream franchise in the United States. A primary factor in its success has been its ability to attract amazing front-line talent. Cold Stone's unique audition process—a departure from the conventional applications and interview process—helps franchisees of this burgeoning brand land talented, outgoing, quick-thinking, energetic teens with a flair for the dramatic and a knack for engaging people. Management takes these young recruits and instills in each of them a passion for delivering "the ultimate ice cream experience."

That's what this confectioner is all about—channeling a raw passion for expression into front-liners who can serve up a great product with charisma and style. Cold Stone's customers not only buy superpremium ice cream and treats; they enter into a multisensory experience involving sight, sound, and smell that makes the product taste even better. This takes more than just good-tasting ice cream in a nice-looking strip mall; it takes enthusiastic young performers. Cold Stone crewmembers have fast become versatile assets who actively contribute to the success of this breakthrough brand.

Cold Stone knows that, to meet its goals, it must get young front-line crew members to appreciate fully the importance of their role and to give a damn about the company and its customers. Although its recipe for ice cream is a secret, its recipe for recruiting, training, and motivating Opies is not. They serve up 11 primary ingredients.

1. Smart hiring. Cold Stone enables crewmembers to participate at a higher level than you find in most other companies that hire teens. From the beginning, Cold Stone Creamery storeowners send the message to kidployees that, "What you think counts." No matter which side of the stage they are on, these teens know that their input is valued and needed. In the audition process, for example, seasoned crewmembers serve as judges, along with the store's owner and managers. What they think and do determines the success of the store.

Cold Stone's five core values—do the right thing, win as a team, be the best . . . be number one, profit by making people happy, and bring out the best in our people—permeate the culture and serve as the guiding force behind every action and decision. In a word: *empowerment.* Management wants to make certain to attract and hire workers who are ready to be empowered.

2. Training to win. Cold Stone is committed to training, training, *and training some more.* They've developed a library of in-store computer-based training (CBT) modules. Crewmembers can sit down and, as schedules allow, complete a series of custom-created training programs. The CBT modules use clever titles and inside jargon such as "Mix Master: Romancing the Stone," "Defusing 'Bombs' and Other Explosive Situations," "Ice Cream Love 101," and "Edu-cake-tion." Through this training, crewmembers not only learn how the company operates, they're schooled on delivering excellent customer service, food safety, store operations, current promotions, and so on. The CBT modules are numerous, short, stimulating, and interactive; they can be completed in any sequence. New modules are created frequently and sent to stores to keep young talent learning and growing.

3. Training to win II. Cold Stone also creates CBT modules for franchisees and managers to help them run their businesses and support the Cold Stone culture. From the first day of Ice Cream University—the intense two-week course that franchisees are required to attend before opening their stores—owners learn about the attitudes and values of today's youth and the huge role they'll play in the success of their stores.

The idea is to train franchisees how to deal with common management problems, while teaching them specialized skills such as "How to Conduct an Audition." The CBT modules keep store operators up to speed on the mechanics of making ice cream and maintaining the equipment and also offer ideas and strategies to help them maximize their crew. Franchisees come to realize that, in the end, much of their day-to-day operation rests in the hands of the teens who are the face of the their brand.

4. Opportunity abounds. Front-line jobs at Cold Stone are complex. Duties include everything from greeting customers and making the sale to taking inventory and handling all the ice cream production. It's that complexity, though, that creates the challenges kidployees find so irresistible.

By comparison, many other jobs available to this labor group have a smaller scope and limit kidployees to one or two main functions. The range of responsibilities required of Cold Stone crewmembers, plus the huge expectations, is a sure-fire formula for creating pride and motivation, especially for an Opie.

Teens in this company feel proud of their accomplishments. They know they are empowered to make critical decisions every day, and that empowerment strengthens their interest in taking on more—and doing more—better.

5. Empathetic to teen lifestyle. Cold Stone goes out of its way to be flexible with its crewmembers, taking a real-world approach to its crewmembers' personal lives and individual schedules. Schedules fit to their worlds, not necessarily the other way around. If one crewmember plays football, for example, his manager might allow him to be on hiatus during the season, or perhaps only work on Sunday afternoons during the season. As a result, turnover is lower, morale is higher, and Cold Stone wins in ways that add up.

6. Freedom of expression. Many quick-service restaurants operate under a process-driven system in which everyone is taught to do the same things, offer the same greetings, and act in the same way. You know the drill: you walk into a store, the clerk gives you a predictable greeting such as, "Welcome, may I take your order?" and you respond robotically with, "Yes, I'll have a burger and fries." In a process-driven system like this, workers merely plug in information; it's all linear with no room for personal expression and random play.

Cold Stone Creamery determined long ago that the *creativity* and *individuality* of an "ultimate crew" would vastly differentiate the company from all other ice cream vendors. Cold Stone understood that the magic occurs in recognizing crewmembers' distinctive personalities, unique strengths, and talents. So Cold Stone took the process (because, yes, there must still be processes) and drew a face on it! They created room in the process for crew members to express their passion and pride—to become enthusiastic brand ambassadors.

Cold Stone crewmembers build the brand by delivering ultimate ice cream experiences every day, achieving this by expressing their own creativity while exploring their customers' palate. Crewmembers plug into their own personalities to

- determine if the customer has been there before.
- ask if the customer has a favorite flavor of ice cream (always a great ice breaker—who doesn't want to share that?).
- give them a taste of the ice cream flavor (made fresh daily, they point out).
- suggest a winning combination of ice cream flavors, cookies, candies, pie fillings, fruits, or nuts.

This dialog opens up lines of communication with a customer that puts the "Do you want fries with that?" conversation to shame. Why? Because, through this dialog, crewmembers create and deliver ultimate ice cream experiences—and they know it!

7. Rewarding performance and individuality. In addition to hourly wages, management uses contests to encourage more sales (e.g., crewmembers who sell the most waffle products or ice cream mix-ins during a one-hour period win movie tickets or "premium" shift schedules for the following week). But Cold Stone also invites the customer to reward front-liners who have gone beyond the norm in delivering the ultimate ice cream experience. On the counter of a Cold Stone Creamery, you'll likely see a tip jar with clever note taped to it saying something like, "Drop a dollar and watch us holler!" When a customer drops in a tip, crewmembers acknowledge the customer, usually in the form of a group sing-a-long performance. The kidployees love to do this, and the customers love to watch—making it a self-perpetuating formula for fun, showmanship, and service.

Additional monetary incentives speak to crewmembers, yet spot incentives say more than higher wages. Real incentives lie in crewmembers being able to recognize the power of their own actions related to customer satisfaction and increased revenue. It doesn't take long for them to see the correlation between delighting the customer and personal cash flow. That's how the front line directly connects to the bottom line.

Through the service experience—including tips and the sung acknowledgments—crewmembers learn that they have control over the quality of their work experience, the quality of every customer's experience, and their take-home pay. They clearly learn to give a damn as they complete this cycle: crew delivers exceptional customer service, crew is rewarded, and the legend of Cold Stone expands. Everyone wins!

8. Coaching teamwork. During training for new crewmembers, management takes one-on-one face time to explain how taxes are taken out, how paychecks are computed, and how raises are given. Because this job is likely the kidployees' first, the managers make certain they address all questions from the beginning.

Then, in many stores, the rest of the core skills training is provided by an experienced crewmember who has completed all certifications and core skills training programs. That peer is known as a "coach." Coaches usually receive an increase in pay, but wearing the distinctive shirt that goes along with the title seems to get more mileage than getting cash in their "race to be cool."

9. Celebrating contribution. I spoke at Cold Stone Creamery's national convention in Las Vegas in 2003 and had an intensive, first-hand experience with Cold Stone. I learned how they truly value their front-line kidployees. Teen employees from Cold Stone Creameries across the country attended seminars and participated in the "Waffle Bowl"—a competition based upon ice cream knowledge, mix mastery, and showmanship skills. This team competition pits crews against each other for special recognition, prizes, and awards. The main stage event culminated in the crowning of a winning—and very proud—crew of Cold Stone mix masters.

Further programs are underway to offer scholarships and additional specialized training and recognition for outstanding crewmembers. All these efforts support Cold Stone's journey toward creating the "best first job" experience for every crewmember—an experience that crew and parent alike are beginning to recognize as nothing short of a must-have experience for any teen.

10. Train to retain. Cold Stone is in business for the long haul. Managers realize that if they consistently strive to be the "best first job," the company and its crewmembers will be rewarded in other ways. Many of these crewmembers will go on to college and come back as store managers or possibly as team members at The Creamery (the "cooler than *Corporate* or *HQ*" term used to describe Cold Stone's home offices in Scottsdale).

As many crew members go on to careers in other fields, they'll discover that the life skills they used at "that fun ice cream job" will serve them and support their success. And these successful professionals of the future will show their loyalty as Cold Stone customers. They'll bring their friends and, when they get married, they'll bring their spouses and, eventually, their kids.

Ha, you say; that's the long, *long* haul. How can Cold Stone be focused on that? The answer is that the company believes in the long-term future and viability in the company and the company's greatest asset: its one-of-a-kind crewmembers.

11. Perpetuate the species. Cold Stone knows that by holding onto quality crew members as long as possible—whether it's longer by a week, a month, or a season—the benefits are huge. When those crewmembers are passionate about their jobs and the ice cream concoctions they create, and when they look forward to delighting customers, they raise the probability that customers will come back, raising the profitability of each store. Customers talk to other customers, and soon the store has built a strong reputation locally. Eventually, someone from the media hears the buzz, and the store gets coverage. Media exposure creates a following, too, and soon, the manager can predict a healthy stream of sales revenue. Customers start to incorporate the store into their lives. They even put the store's phone number into their cell phones, so they can quickly order Cold Stone ice cream cakes for all occasions. The store becomes institutionalized within the community, becoming the automatic choice when people want ice cream.

This growing company has seen the above pattern unfold again and again. No doubt it happens in great part because of the super premium ice cream, but that's only the half of it; the huge successes Cold Stone experiences wouldn't be possible without a passionate group of young front-liners minding the store.

Pass the Passion, Please

To be sure, these discoveries aren't new; some of the crew-related strategies that Cold Stone employs were offered as early as 20 years ago by chains such as Chuck E. Cheese's. Cold Stone has merely made the commitment to incorporate "all things ultimate" into every initiative, every goal—both short term and long term—to signal to crewmembers that, "This place is different, and you are part of something special." Like Disney and other companies that have taken similar steps to support their culture, Cold Stone knows that every little bit contributes to creating a culture that's palpable to customers and crew alike.

Suppose you're reading this while managing some other type of store that perhaps doesn't have the obviously teen-friendly culture of Cold Stone. You still have options. Even incorporating a tiny fraction of what Cold Stone does could make a difference in your ability to attract, recruit, and retain excellent front-line employees. So ask yourself, "How regimented do we need to be in our processes? Can we allow some of our talented teen employees to add their unique input in some way? Can we seek their input in decision making? Where can we offer some slack? Where can they insert their personalities into the equation?"

Doing Something Right

Cold Stone takes a vested interest in each crewmember; it doesn't simply ask that crewmembers take a vested interest in them. When managers invest time, energy, and money into employees, they send a message that crewmembers and their parents can't deny and one that sticks with me, too: Cold Stone is doing something right.

This company clearly cares about its crewmembers and conscientiously recognizes their accomplishments and contributions. Cold Stone acknowledges that the skills learned and experiences gained working there can positively influence the future success of a kidployee. These efforts make Cold Stone the employer of choice for *future employees*. Having "Cold Stone" on a résumé is a testament to a young candidate's confidence, interpersonal skills, dependability, and responsibility.

> Crewmembers get invested in Cold Stone's success because they know they're offering an ice cream experience that customers can't find anywhere else. As these crew-based programs develop and evolve, no doubt these kidployees will continue to give a damn. It's all about infusing every effort with passion, mixed with a little bit of play and a lot of personality. The result is bound to be remarkable, unexpected, and irresistible.

19

OPPORTUNITY KNOCKS
AT SOUTHWESTERN

We build people. And those people are building a great company.

The Southwestern Company

This statement is not only The Southwestern Company's tagline; this core belief has made this company one of most successful employers of college students in the history of the United States.

Based in Nashville, Tennessee, Southwestern has been in business since 1855, when Nashville was regarded as a city in the southwest, not the southeast as it is today. The Southwestern Company does one thing and one thing only: it sells educational reference books to families door to door.

The Volume Library, its incredible flagship offering, consists of a set of three large books covering 44 school subjects in each grade level from kindergarten through 12. The Library includes preparation material and sample college entrance examinations. Like "encyclopedias on steroids," each subject features comprehensive how-to examples, so parents and kids can always find the help they need. For many parents with school-aged children, these books aren't considered a luxury; they're a must.

No set of books like The Volume Library is produced anywhere else in the world. You can't buy it online, you can't order it through a catalogue, and you can't pick it up in a bookstore. There's only one way to acquire these books—directly from a college student and only during the summer months. Imagine the recruitment effort that takes!

Think You Have It Tough?

Instead of recruiting kidployees to your present company, suppose you're asked to recruit a staff of 3,500 kids from 350 college students throughout the United States, Canada, and Europe.

In a nutshell, here's what the 3,000+ seasonal jobs require:

Southwestern sales reps sell books door to door, on straight commission, with no base salary. If selected, student recruits must travel to Nashville at their own expense and attend one week of intensive sales training, unpaid, at their own expense. At the completion of this training, the rep will be working in their own sales area hundreds of miles from home for the duration of the summer.

Upon arrival in their assigned locale, the reps need to secure a place to live for the summer. One way they accomplish this is by knocking on doors until they find a family who will rent them a room for the summer. The rep won't be home much, though.

The suggested daily regimen is vigorous. Monday through Saturday, the sales reps awaken at 6:00 AM and take a chilly, invigorating shower. They get dressed, eat breakfast, do calisthenics, take in some motivational material, and head out to knock on the first door no later than 7:59 AM. Their lunch break consists of eating a peanut butter and jelly sandwich as they walk between houses. The reps knock on the last door of the day at 8:59 PM. After that last presentation, they return to their home base to make dinner, complete paperwork, and prepare for the following day. Student reps work the entire summer, averaging an 80-hour week, with no time off for summer holidays, family vacations, or birthdays. On Sundays, they meet with other reps in their vicinity for a weekly sales meeting followed by afternoon recreation. That evening, they return home to do laundry and chill out before the next week begins.

Comparatively speaking, finding an Opie for your business seems like a walk in the park, doesn't it? Yet surprisingly, even with today's breed of kidployee comprising 100 percent of its front line, Southwestern's sales have never been stronger. Its leaders believe the pool of young talent has never been deeper.

Building Character and Bank Accounts

You must be thinking, "What kind of degenerate, money-grubbing, totally desperate college kid would take a job like this? Would you believe top students from renowned universities like Harvard, Stanford, and Duke? Southwestern has become a magnet for the best and the brightest—remarkable young people wanting to be challenged and seeking to grow. Southwestern alumni have gone on to become top execs for *Fortune* 500 companies, leading entrepreneurs, and governors and Supreme Court justices.

College students are attracted to this opportunity because of the tremendous income potential with no ceiling on their earnings. Most reps who survive the summer pocket significantly more than the typical college student who works in construction and retail. No guarantees come with the territory, however, and the high income is not why most student reps choose this path.

Each student rep, acting as an independent contractor, must pay for their own living expenses and manage their own personal finances. For many, this entrée into entrepreneurship helps them tackle the real world of business head-on. Their Southwestern experience on a résumé jumps out to headhunters and future employers, giving them a leg up on competing peers after graduation. Consider this: All 20-year-olds who have successfully operated their own businesses, worked 80-hour weeks, and overcome the kind of rejection these young people have encountered can handle just about anything that's thrown at them.

But this doesn't tell the complete story.

Ask Southwestern managers what their company does, and they'll say, "We build character; we just happen to sell books." Southwestern declares that no other summer job in the world will have a greater positive impact on a young person's life. And I have become a steadfast believer. Here's why.

My son worked as a sales rep for Southwestern last summer, and I can assure you that the kid I sent to Nashville in May wasn't the same one who came home in August. Zac, age 20, grew from a boy to a man in 90 days.

Although he's a great kid and a dean's list student, Zac had never been drawn toward hard work, long days, or personal rejection. The fact that he learned to sprint willingly and knowingly toward all three fascinated me. Even though he called me many times on the verge of tears and wanting to quit, he hung in there and made it through to the last day. Although he's accomplished a lot in his young life, Zac prizes his Southwestern experience above anything he has ever done—and plans to return for his second summer in May.

HOW DOES SOUTHWESTERN GET THEM TO GIVE A DAMN?

How can this company have such remarkable appeal to Zac and thousands of others? How can Southwestern continue, year after year, to attract and retain huge numbers of extremely talented kids, while other companies offering guaranteed income and benefits and lots of flexibility turn them off?

The answers lie in Southwestern's refusal to deviate from these five time-honored principles and values.

#1. Honesty. In a world where they have so often been deceived, young people are drawn to those who shoot straight with no bull and zero hype.

Southwestern recruiters never sugarcoat the job to entice an applicant. They let students know at the onset it will be the hardest work they've ever done; they warn them that, on many occasions, they'll feel like giving up.

Before the summer begins, the managers ask participants to sign a document that details 66 hard, cold facts about this job. Further, they tell their recruits many times before they report to training (and again while in training) that doors will be slammed in their faces and they'll certainly encounter nasty people. They warn the recruits that they'll walk many miles through neighborhoods in blistering heat and humidity, even when it's dark, windy, chilly, and rainy. They also warn them to anticipate feeling hungry, tired, and homesick every single day.

Knowing the necessity of getting buy in from parents, Southwestern managers also form crucial alliances and strong bonds with each recruit's parents. Zac's supervisor Rory—a college student older than Zac by only one year—also knocks on doors as a rep. Before Zac was officially selected, Rory came to our house and told my wife and me, "After a few weeks, Zac will call you and beg to come home. Be expecting that call." As predicted, the call came, and we were prepared to respond by listening to him and encouraging him. By the way, during one summer, Rory earned more than most teachers, with 15 years of experience and a master's degree, earn in a year. He is and was, beyond question, the most polished and professional 21-year-old kid we've ever met.

#2. Challenge. They appear to be looking for easy money—a simple, cushy, mindless job—when they really want to be challenged to the extreme limits of their potential.

Many Baby Boomers are under the mistaken impression that today's "inherently lazy" kidployees would rather play video games than work. In reality, the opposite is true. America bursts with young people attracted to the daunting challenge and adventure presented by Southwestern. Perhaps because they've heard their parents describe how much more difficult they had it when they were young ("I walked to school every day, five miles, uphill, in waist-high snow . . . ."), they want to test their own metal. Maybe they find it appealing to attempt something that their friends find "unreal" and "totally psycho." Or it could be they are tired of having everything they've ever wanted handed to them; they're yearning for the opportunity to slay a mighty dragon, run to a mountain top, and scream, "Look out world! I am here, and I'm a force to be reckoned with!" Whatever the reason, the tremendous challenge that a summer of knocking on doors presents doesn't *repel* today's youth; it *compels* them.

#3. Leadership. Many Boomers think that kids today resist rules, structure, and authority. In reality, they've grown up in a relaxed society that has left them thirsty for discipline and principled leadership.

Every kid has heard the cliché, "Don't just talk the talk, walk the walk!" But at Southwestern, this edict is personified. Except for the support staff in the Nashville headquarters, everyone who works for the Southwestern Company started out as a door-to-door sales rep. Even the president, Jerry Heffel, began his career with Southwestern as a student rep at Oklahoma State University.

Kidployees readily buy in to a tough assignment when they know that those giving them the assignment have also served on the front line and tackled similar challenges. This doesn't mean they want to hear old war stories, but they do feel more connected to leaders who have battle scars from time spent on the front line. Conversely, those whose experience comes only from books or from jobs in unrelated fields are often quickly pegged as "posers" who can be taken less seriously.

Because college kids respect the hands-on experience of their Southwestern managers, they eagerly accept direction from them, even more so than they would from an instructor or someone with a PhD. Sales reps take cold showers at 6:00 AM because they know that their manager takes one, too. They don't resent the rigid structure the company has in place because they're given an explanation for the difficult tasks they're required to do. Southwestern doesn't believe in managing from behind the desk; its leaders make themselves available to help, advise, console, and motivate. As a result, their front-line reps buy in and have no problem taking direction.

#4. Opportunity Consistently demonstrate (through story and example) how short-term sacrifice leads to long-term growth and prosperity. Help your young talent understand that the key to success lies in the fusion of skills, character, and experience. In this job, they'll be attracted to opportunities that present a chance for the development of all three.

Members of your front line may seem only to focus on the present, not the future. Yet most of them realize they need more than a classroom education to succeed in a global marketplace. That's why Southwestern emphasizes to students how their experience will make them valuable to prospective employers in every industry. The combination of attitudes and skills that become deeply ingrained in those who complete this comprehensive summer program are extremely rare and highly desirable. Merrill Lynch, Edward D. Jones, and Prudential are among the large companies who routinely seek out Southwestern alumni.

As they arrive in Nashville for training, new reps walk the halls of the company headquarters, where they can't help but notice the portraits of past reps who've gone on to achieve great things. Luminaries from business, education, sports, music, and politics are prominently featured. To a 20-year-old who might have felt lost or confused on a crowded college campus, who might be searching for a way to launch a career, this imagery boldly says, "This is your opportunity to begin a great future!"

#5. Recognition. The older we get, the more we want to be acknowledged for our efforts. Nothing feels better than a pat on the back from someone we respect and love.

Five-year-olds get to see almost every drawing they do displayed prominently on their refrigerator doors at home. Yet, when those kids become engineering students, they could design a complete water treatment plant without their parents ever knowing. Children grow, but no one ever outgrows a need for praise and acknowledgment.

Recognizing their young employees for their accomplishments is big at Southwestern. Very big. Although the company hosts a fall awards banquet inviting parents to see their kids receive plaques, pins, watches, trips, and cool merchandise, they don't wait until year-end to recognize effort and accomplishment. Throughout the summer selling season, students receive weekly awards, prizes, and calls from district managers congratulating them for reaching milestones. No sales rep, even one who struggles, gets left unappreciated for more than a few days. Managers always single out positive things in their recruits and lavish praise on them. Because no amount of effort is taken for granted, many young people finish the summer program knowing they'll be exalted just for doing so.

Rare Values

Honesty. Challenge. Leadership. Opportunity. Recognition. Rare values in today's world, especially from the vantage point of a college kid looking for a summer job. But Southwestern's history of consistently attracting, developing, and retaining top talent hasn't come by accident. The company doesn't make changes to boost sales or decrease expenses if it means compromising on any of its 150-year-old values. In this case, *not changing* proves to be a refreshing change.

20

U.S. ARMY: BUY IN
OF THE HIGHEST ORDER

In this day of mercenary résumé builders, tumultuous employee turnover, corporate upheaval, and the free agent mentality among kidployees, how can you convince your front-liners to buy in to your company's mission? I mean buy in of the highest order— to the degree that they'd forgo much better pay and working conditions elsewhere and even put their life on the line for your organization.

Sounds implausible if not impossible, right? Why, then, do young men and women continue to enlist in the U.S. Army in record numbers, especially during a time of bloody conflict in the Middle East and protests against military involvement across the nation? Even with terrorists and insurgents grabbing headlines every day, the U.S. Army still meets its recruiting goals.

Take a moment to realize that, when the Army enlists its recruits, it's not merely getting buy in on the job—the tour of duty—but also buy in that affects a significant chunk of their lives. The Army dictates where they live, how they dress, to whom they report, and even what they eat. They actually buy in to an entire lifestyle—with the added possibility that they'll get killed on the job.

Dressing in drab green and possibly fighting in a distant land in a controversial war? Who wants to take on that less than glamorous job? Yet the U.S. Army proudly boasts of attracting high-caliber, high-quality kids and has made tremendous gains in recruitment in recent years.

In 2004, the U.S. Army set a goal to recruit 77,000 new active troops and 21,200 reserve troops, ending up with slightly more than these numbers. This was the fifth straight year the Army met its goal, which is set by Congress each year.

Douglas Smith, spokesperson for the Army Recruiting Command at Fort Knox, Kentucky, said, "Our recruiting stayed successful after 9/11. We've also stayed successful leading into the buildup into the war in Iraq and during the war, too. We're not overly concerned."

The Army's latest goal for future recruiting has risen to 80,000 new active Army soldiers and 22,175 Army reservists—its four-year plan is to boost overall troop strength by 30,000. Of those, 20,000 are expected to come through its recruiting efforts and 10,000 more from reenlistments.

How has the Army kept these numbers so high? Is it the signing bonus or the college tuition reimbursement program? Is it the coolness of the "hip" camouflage uniform? Is it because, in today's economy, a good job is darn hard to find?

None of the above, according to Dennis Cavin, commanding general of the U.S. Army's recruiting and basic training programs (termed *Accessions*). General Cavin shed light on this intriguing mystery over dinner one evening at Fort Leonard Wood, Missouri.

APPEAL TO CORE VALUES

"When we asked 11,000 recruits aged 17 to 21 why they were enlisting in the Army, the signing bonus and tuition reimbursement came low on the list," General Cavin told me. "Turns out, the youth of our great nation want desperately to belong to something bigger than themselves." So much so, apparently, that they willingly go to battle for it.

Kids who join the Army want to make a difference. They want assurance that they're doing something worthwhile and contributing to the greater good. They possess a sense of loyalty, patriotism, and duty. The burgeoning number of Army recruits—especially when it's so easy to find a job that pays more and requires less—proves that the values they hold could be grossly underestimated.

FULL DISCLOSURE

Visit the official Army recruiting Web site (http://www.goarmy.com), and you'll see that no effort is made to paint a rosy picture of what lies ahead. Because the Army wants recruits to know exactly what they're signing up for, it presents a detailed view of each of the nine weeks of boot camp.

The objectives are outlined and the language is clear: week one, fall in; week two, direction; week three, endurance; etc. The photos depict hard work, tough training, and grueling conditions. The blunt photo captions state things like, "One thing you'll realize in week three is to believe in the mantra: mind over matter. Physical and mental challenges build as you start simulated combat drills."

General Cavin regularly visits with young soldiers during their brutal days of boot camp. "I tell them I'm the guy who signed their enlistment contracts and ask them if they want to back out of the deal." So far, he's never had a taker. "They seem to know exactly what they're getting themselves into. We don't paint a pretty picture to get them to join. We're brutally honest, and these kids gravitate toward that.

"As an example, I asked a young soldier whom I passed in the Louisville airport why he joined the Army, and he told me that he'd rather die for something he believed in than live for something that he didn't."

General Cavin said they also gravitate toward basic values like honor and integrity, citing that the Army trains young people to do what's right, legally and morally. If you compare these values to the plethora of contradictory messages coming from sports, advertising, popular music, and reality television, it becomes easier to understand why the Army has become an attractive alternative.

GANG GREEN

"Be all you can be." This was the advertising slogan used to attract Baby Boomer soldiers in the '70s and '80s. It spoke to the mindset of a generation that placed a high value on self and wanted to develop skills that would propel their careers. Contrast that slogan to the Army's current recruiting tagline, "An army of one," and you'll see how the focus has shifted from *me* to *we*. The new slogan implies a sense of team, unity, and family, while the old one appealed to individual goals.

Quite obviously, the Army's marketing people understand that today's young people want to be a part of a community. Whether because so many have come from weak nuclear families or because they're tired of being connected to others via fiber optics, recruits are intrigued by the idea of forming lifelong bonds with others.

Army leaders also know full well that today's kidployees—their soldiers—aren't willing to die for their country as many of their counterparts of previous eras would. However odd it might sound, they're willing to die for their friends, particularly their friends in the foxhole—the soldiers serving with them. "They feel a vital connection to the person who covers their back," General Cavin said.

The Army recognizes that today's youth don't want to go it alone. Its leaders invite recruits to bring a friend along to get the most out of the Army adventure and to have a friend to lean on in tough times. They know that when recruits recruit their friends, their commitment level grows stronger, and they will each serve longer. They also realize that it's easier to follow through on a difficult assignment when giving up means more than being disappointed in yourself but also letting down a trusted friend.

Soldiers endure basic training together before being shipped out to faraway places, where they come to rely on each other even more. In many respects, the bonds formed are similar to those found among urban gang members whose credo is, "We're brothers for life." Some come from wealthy homes where they had plenty of stuff but little face time with mom or dad. Others come from broken homes where no one cared about them. But the common denominator is that they all want to belong to something that offers strength and unity with a purpose.

The new breed of young soldier wants to wear the uniform that's worn by others like them—peers having the same experiences and loyalties they do in the face of danger. Most importantly, Army recruits are lured by the promise of a familial love, something they might not have received—or got too little of—growing up.

ADRENALIN FIX

Like a magnet, today's 16- to 24-year-olds are drawn toward excitement and repelled by anything that smacks of sameness. "The Army may get a bad rap for being a lot of things," a colonel told me, "but boring ain't on the list!"

According to the National Institute of Media and Family, 80 percent of all kids aged 2 to 17 have a computer in their home, and 92 percent of those same kids have regular access to video games. Gaming is a billion-dollar industry. The tens of thousands of different games all come prepackaged with high-speed graphics and an adrenalin rush. This makes it impossible to wow a kidployee who's conditioned to constant, ever-changing excitement with an assembly line-type job.

To many young people, joining the U.S. military means experiencing life at the intersection of speed and surprise—an exciting place to be. The U.S. Navy's recruiting tagline is, "Accelerate your life," and their ads ask this question: "If your life was a book, would anyone want to read it?" The U.S. Air Force labels each of its 150 jobs/careers as "missions." And the U.S. Marines are only looking for "the few, the proud."

Many kidployees find adventure irresistible. The desire to see, to go, and to do compels them to enlist in the armed services. While some companies and organizations try to lure potential recruits by saying, "No two days are the same," the army guarantees to deliver on that promise.

TAKE-AWAY IDEAS FROM THE U.S. ARMY

In your business, what ideas can you borrow from U.S. Army recruiters about employing kidployees? Consider these:

- Don't believe the stereotyping buzz claiming that our kids are only out for themselves and that they don't value service and loyalty. The recruiting success of the U.S. Army proves that this generation has a strong sense of purpose. Let them see your mission statement.
- Loyalty is an even exchange, not a one-sided transaction. Don't expect buy in from your young talent if your organization is shallow in purpose and focused only on profits. Not that making money is a bad thing, but kidployees want to know they're part of an organization that also makes a worthwhile contribution to society.
- Strive for 100 percent honesty in every phase of your operation. Resist the temptation to make an entry-level job, or any job, sound better than it is to fill a vacancy. Doing so might temporarily solve a scheduling dilemma, but you'll stock your front lines with uncommitted troops who will likely abandon ship at the first sign of trouble.
- Understand the high degree of importance your front-liners place on stimulation and change. They want positions that allow them to learn new things and rotate assignments frequently. Never ask your kidployees to do the same thing day in and day out and expect them to remain focused and productive.

- Encourage camaraderie among your front-liners and provide frequent opportunities for them to build relationships away from the workplace. They might never bleed your company colors or recite your mission statement, but they'll go to the wall for the coworkers who help them along the way.
- Kidployees need to know they're working in an environment where teamwork and unity are encouraged and supported, the same way army buddies in a foxhole watch each others' backs. Go out of your way to provide opportunities for your kidployees to bond.

21

A GREAT JOB
FLIPPIN' BURGERS?

"**Y**ou don't want to end up flippin' burgers, do you?" It's always been a left-field slam on a kid's first job. But in eastern Tennessee, *flippin' burgers* isn't necessarily a slam. If you're lucky enough to flip burgers at Pal's Sudden Service, it's an honor.

Pal's chain of 19 quick-service restaurants has generated outrageous results for more than five decades. Until a few years ago, most people outside of eastern Tennessee hadn't heard of Pal's, the unmistakable drive-through burger joints with simulated 25-foot hot dogs, hamburgers, fries, and drink cups attached to their roofs and exteriors. Then in 2001, Pal's was thrust into the national spotlight after it won the prestigious Malcolm Baldrige Award, a congressional award presented annually to five businesses for quality and service. Pal's is the only restaurant ever to win this coveted award, and it didn't come by happenstance.

Over the past decade, Pal's marketing, training, and operations have meshed to create the kind of double-digit growth that most competitors find intimidating. Pal's consistently outperforms national hamburger chains in profit per store, sales per labor hour, health inspections, and customer satisfaction. The company averages

- less than 1 complaint per 1,000 customers and
- less than 1 mistake per 2,000 transactions in order accuracy.

Standing on their front lines are the same kind of kidployees everyone else complains about. However, in its local drawing area, Pal's has developed the reputation among parents as *the* place you send your kids to teach them how to work.

ALL COMPANY-OWNED STORES

All of Pal's locations are company owned. To date, the company has received 7,200 requests for franchising information from interested investors who want Pal's to offer franchises. Each store is an astounding 50 percent more profitable than the industry standard, while employee turnover is less than one third of the norm.

President and CEO Thom Crosby describes his restaurants as a manufacturing concern, like that of Ford Motors. "We bring in raw products and convert them into a unique, branded product you can only get here," he states, adding that Ford makes a specified number of cars in stages while Pal's makes its products as ordered or on demand. He says that melding the education and service businesses are the second and third components of their success. "We get the right people into the company, align them to be a success, and make sure we give them the skills."

A COMMUNITY PARTNER

Pal's supports the communities in which it operates with financial and staff resources at both the corporate and individual store levels. For example, corporate senior leaders are top sponsors of the United Way. At the store level, general managers participate in such community activities as teaching food service and food safety classes at high schools, serving as schools' business partners, donating materials for special events, and sponsoring special community, school, and church events.

The good deeds do more than raise the profile of Pal's to potential customers; they resonate with future kidployees. Children who see Pal's as a friend to their schools, parks, and activities grow into teens who feel inclined to trust the company as an employer.

A WINNING RECIPE

When it comes to inducing heart-and-soul buy in from teenage employees, most of whom are on their first job, Pal's has developed a winning recipe. The primary ingredients for its stores' success include the following:

- Perception of kidployees
- Uncompromising structure
- Perpetual crosstraining
- Wideopen communication
- Total employee empowerment
- Uninterrupted mentorship

Perception of Kidployees

There's an old adage that says, "You may or may not get what you want out of your kids. You may or may not get what you deserve. But you will always get exactly what you expect from them." This core principle at Pal's is the precursor to the company's tremendous success with kids.

Ask most managers around the country to give you their opinion of the quality of their talent pool, and you're likely hear foul language. Not at Pal's. Crosby says his managers don't encounter the problems that other companies experience with today's young employees. "They're the smartest, most creative, best educated workers in history," claims Crosby. "It's a belief widely held by the management at Pal's. We expect the best and we accept nothing less."

Online job candidates at http://www.palsweb.com are greeted by this no-spin message:

> If you want to become a part of a specialized team that sets the highest standards in the restaurant industry, take a look at Pal's. We serve the best quality products with the fastest, friendliest, most accurate service and the cleanest operations. Pal's has become the standard by which others are judged.
>
> We are dedicated to working with and training people who want to become the very best. Pal's has a flexible work schedule and a fun and fast-paced work environment where people can learn, grow, and succeed while earning money.

When teens are greeted with sincere, positive expectancy, they begin to believe they are capable of doing good work. They become trustworthy because they are trusted. They become accountable because they are expected to be.

While kids can often get by with the bare minimum, leaders at Pal's demand top performance from their young front-liners; they don't settle for mediocrity from any of them. They hold teens to the highest standards and treat them as if each is a partner in an effort to make Pal's the best restaurant in the world. For some, it could be the first time anyone ever believed in them.

Uncompromising Structure

Pal's has absolutely no room for personal interpretation of its dress code, attendance policy, or operations procedures. From top to bottom, the organization is run more like a marine barracks than a hamburger joint. With white glove cleanliness, uniforms must be worn to exact standards, even when the employee is off duty or in transit.

No deviations are allowed from Pal's processes. Crosby states, "We are into capturing and replicating creativity, and so we focus on results first. Then we look at standards. If the result is wrong and everyone is doing it right, we realize we designed a bad system." So far, everyone is doing it right—the results are exemplary.

Employees must arrive 15 minutes before their scheduled start time. If they arrive at the scheduled time, they are sent home. No kidding! Every kidployee is expected to know and play by the rules, no exceptions and no deviations. Although this seems counterintuitive to working with today's youth, Pal's firm boundaries draw them in. The company doesn't yield to individual requests or make exceptions for personality styles. Their young talent respects these fair and exacting standards.

Perpetual Crosstraining

The effectiveness of Pal's training has increased at the same rate as its market share, sales growth, and profitability. Pal's uses a four-step model to train its employees—show, do, evaluate, and perform again—and requires employees to demonstrate 100 percent competence before being allowed to work at a specific work station. Such rigor often requires a new hire to repeat a specific training module on the path to proficiency.

Pal's requires in-store training on processes, health and safety, and organizational culture for new staff at all facilities via computer-based training, flash cards, and one-on-one coaching. It also requires cross-training of all store-level staff to ensure a complete understanding of all production and service procedures and quality standards.

"We're the Navy Seals of the restaurant business," Crosby says. "Our training never ends. The 16-year-olds who draw drinks? We want them to know everything about the entire science of carbonation, from proper temperatures to the machine technology. We have cola experts who are the equivalent of wine experts."

At Pal's, employee evaluations don't exclusively rest in the hands of supervisors and managers, because it can be too easy to fool the leader. Based on the idea that peers more closely see an employee's behavior, dedication level, and reaction to pressure than a supervisor, they make the evaluations. This directly relates to the effectiveness of the training program.

Pal's employees are never shown something once. Instead, they get intensely trained on a specific skill, then are given a timed test and expected to achieve a perfect score. The company incorporates a computerized system to track each employee's training regimen and profile. It periodically reminds management that it's once again time, for example, to assess Lawanda's skills at the french fry station. This time, however, Lawanda must not only achieve a perfect score, she must also do it in less time than in her previous assessment.

As a result, every kidployee has to relearn everything about every aspect of the total operation. This rigorous approach eliminates boredom; each new day offers the opportunity to improve on the previous day and move closer to completely mastering an entire process. Crosby insists, "Our success is directly related to the education and training of those who manufacture our products."

Managers are encouraged to help employees based on the results of their quizzes. Once an employee scores a 100, the goal is to maintain that 100 throughout the term of employment. This system helps managers spend more time focused on the bigger picture of their restaurant's opportunities and threats, as well as the main components of their business: education, leadership, and challenging employees. It also makes scheduling easier, because they know that every kidployee can handle any job in the operation.

Wide-Open Communication

Pal's believes that their front-liners who serve in the trenches every day have the best ideas on how to improve processes, products, and services. So they not only ask for their kidployees' opinions, they insist on receiving them. As a condition of employment, front-liners must routinely submit ideas for improving the operation. Talk about keeping a kid feeling valued!

When a kidployee's idea is implemented, that person's name is recorded in the company archives. They are noted as the originator of the idea, and no one else will be able to take credit for it. Often, the new technique, idea, or strategy gets named after the kid who created it. The originator also receives a commensurate cash award, which encourages the employee—and their coworkers—to keep generating usable ideas.

Idea sharing is so much a part of the Pal's culture that all 762 employees have Thom Crosby's personal cell phone number. They are welcome to call him 24/7. They're told that Crosby keeps his cell phone on his nightstand and is always ready to listen to what his kidployees have to say.

Amazingly, the full contact information including name, address, phone, and e-mail address of all general managers for all locations is also prominently posted on the company Web site. This accessibility strongly indicates the degree to which they make themselves available and accountable. Although Pal's occasionally experiences front-line turnover, it's unlikely for people to leave Pal's because they felt that no one listened to them or their opinions weren't valued.

Total Employee Empowerment

Pal's doesn't want managers to solve problems for front-line staff. If a Pal's customer doesn't like the way a hamburger has been cooked, the 16-year-old handling the complaint is authorized to cook another one for the customer, comp them an entire meal, or offer to cater a birthday party for that customer's child. No manager will question the decision.

Pal's trains all employees in an eight-step, problem-solving formula and empowers them to solve problems on their own. Crosby starts with the belief that their young employees are the smartest people on the planet and follows up by training them continually on every phase of the operation. "You've got to let go and trust them to make decisions," he says.

When today's kidployees feel trusted and empowered rather than belittled and micromanaged, they rise to meet those expectations. Their talent comes shining through when they can innovate and completely buy in.

Uninterrupted Mentorship

If you were a new employee at Pal's, your first day would begin with a 90-minute, face-to-face orientation with your store's general manager, who would hand you a pocketsize booklet. The manager would go over its contents about the company's history, highlighting where Pal's has been, where it is now, where it's going, and—this is critical—how you fit into the overall picture.

Most companies make the mistake of boring their kidployees to tears with corporate materials without ever connecting that information meaningfully to the new kidployees and communicating precisely where they fit in. As a new kidployee at Pal's, your general manager would introduce you to the rules and make certain that you clearly understood the consequences of not strictly adhering to them. After the 90-minute orientation, you would *not* be handed over to a company trainer. Instead, the general manager would be your trainer, mentor, and coach *throughout your employment.*

LOOK MA, NO LAYERS

While Pal's has ridiculously low turnover on the front line, management turnover is virtually nonexistent. There is no layer of management between general manager and Crosby, and general managers are so well compensated, they simply don't leave. To the front line, that means consistency—something extremely rare among food service and retail sectors.

Rather than being "here today and gone tomorrow," Pal's managers and employees have time to develop deep relationships. This creates a kind of stability that nurtures trust and spawns competency and longevity.

22

AND ONE TO GROW ON

It has been said that an idea without implementation leads to stagnation. If you're determined to get your front-liners to care about your bottom line, you need more than insights and philosophies; you need to put a plan into motion.

This book has provided an in-depth understanding of your emerging front-line employees and how best to connect with them. It's given you a picture of what contributions Opie-like kidployees can make. It's also provided examples, profiles, and case studies from a variety of companies and organizations.

As you've read the chapters, perhaps you've found yourself saying, "Yeah well, it may have worked for XYZ, but that would never work in my business." But before you totally dismiss an idea, I suggest examining if you could adapt any part of the idea to your unique situation. The point is: Don't look at what *won't* work; find those things that *can* work.

Here are some quick-hitting ideas to keep your mind churning and your internal "idea factory" open. The companies noted in this chapter have implemented plans to thwart the high level of turnover, perpetuate excellence, and encourage advancement within their respective ranks.

If you spot an idea that's ripe for the picking among the following best practice examples (or from any discussed earlier in the book), I encourage you to adapt it—not adopt it. Today's kidployees prize originality and loathe sameness, so put your own spin on what others do to avoid being seen as a duplicator or an also-ran.

RECRUITMENT/HIRING STRATEGIES

"Greetings," Mr. Spock, the pointy-eared Vulcan of *Star Trek* fame said, "I am pleased to see that we are different. May we together become greater than the sum of both of us." Because recruiting and hiring workers has become an art form, the changing face of the up-and-coming workforce demands *Star Trek*–like diversity in recruitment strategies as well as a need to integrate Baby Boomers and Gen-Xers with the new kidployee component. A number of companies have implemented groundbreaking staffing ideas such as the following:

- Kidployee applicants at Monarch Ski & Snowboard Area in southwestern Colorado don't get a call from a manager. The first person they hear from, almost immediately, is a peer. Monarch has decided that the best people to connect with prospective kidployees are other committed kidployees—a practice that immediately puts the applicant at ease. The front-line staff member can address any concerns from the perspective of the applicant and communicate the pros and the cons of the job. If the applicant has a question a kidployee can't answer, they are referred to management or human resources.
- One might say it's a "trade-off" at Trader Joe's, a specialty grocer with stores throughout the United States. Employees are hired at about $4 an hour more than average retail pay, but in turn are carefully selected because they have cheerful, happy attitudes and know how to move groceries and keep customers coming back for more. This in itself boosts the company's profit margins. Management views its front-line employees as the "soul of Trader Joe's."
- Burger King kidployees are presented with "Burger Bucks" when they recruit other front-liners. The valued Burger Bucks can be redeemed for gift certificates at local vendors.
- Wal-Mart has recruited many Students in Free Enterprise (SIFE) participants into its stores and clubs over the years. SIFE is a global, nonprofit organization that offers students ways to develop leadership, teamwork, and communication skills through learning, practicing, and teaching the principles of free enterprise.

- PetsMart conducts interviews on the sales floor, allowing store managers to study how potential employees interact with customers, part of its Customer Service Unleashed program.
- Whole Foods, a coast-to-coast grocery store, distinguishes itself from its peers by offering a "no secrets" management style. Before being permanently employed, new hires must be voted in by two-thirds of their prospective peers.
- Wieden+Kennedy, a forward-thinking advertising agency in Portland, Oregon, ran a different kind of classified ad in the paper.

> Talented/Directionless, with $/Time to spare? An open call to misfits, oddballs, and wayward youth.

The ad drew more than 3,000 people to the company's Web site. The application's instructions?

> Tell us your story . . . Charm us. Surprise us. Seduce us.

The company believes they found 12 of the most talented creative minds in the country through this unorthodox approach to recruiting.

- The Learn and Earn program developed by Wells Fargo in Orange County, California, attracts part-time tellers wanting some control over their compensation. As tellers complete training modules and case studies, they become more valuable to the bank and subsequently advance through the three tiers of the program, until they reach Expert Teller status. Each tier not only increases a kidployee's hourly wage but also opens more options for a career path within Wells Fargo.
- At Kahala Corporation, a franchising and marketing company for numerous quick-service restaurants, employees are hired at $1.50 to $2.00 above minimum wage. In addition, they receive a $1.00 raise for exhibiting the Kahala Value System that incorporates customer importance, service, product quality, cleanliness, and concern and respect for people. Existing employees receive a $100 bonus for each successful employee referral.
- Fast-food giant Taco Bell's commitment to the community helps attract and retain top employees and improves employee morale. It accomplishes this through its TEENSupreme program, which provides at-risk young people opportunities to develop self-esteem and leadership skills in a safe environment with the support of a well-trained and dedicated staff. In addition to providing grants to local Boys and Girls Clubs of America to start or enhance existing

programs, TEENSupreme raises money to develop and execute character and leadership development, career exploration, and job readiness programs for its 3,100 clubs nationwide.

- Thirty schools from three counties currently participate in the United Parcel Service's (UPS) School to Work program in Louisville, Kentucky. The program gives high school seniors an opportunity to gain valuable work experience as well as earn college credits by taking preliminary college courses. The School to Work program serves as a feeder program for Metropolitan College (a virtual university facilitated by UPS), the University of Louisville, and Jefferson Community College and Technical College. This program offers students a free college education and a part-time job at UPS, where they receive a benefits package that includes health coverage, a 401(k) plan, vacation pay, and a starting salary of $8.50 an hour. UPS pays half the tuition fee and the state pays the other half.

- Ikea, the Swedish furniture maker, is experimenting with a new approach to finding young talented employees: attracting applicants with handwritten ads on the walls of public bathrooms. On its initial try, the company received 60 applications, 4 to 5 times more than what Ikea would have received from a normal newspaper ad. As a bonus, this unusual campaign was significantly cheaper than running a newspaper ad.

TRAINING

Effective leadership spawns effective followership. And a primary tool of followership is training. Several major national vendors have built valuable training programs into their regimen to instill retention and employee loyalty. Here are some examples:

- Within its corporate accounting and finance departments, the video retailer Blockbuster offers a program to develop its future leaders. Blockbuster Leadership and Skills Training (BLAST) is a challenging, 24-month program that involves on-the-job skills training as well as leadership and professional development. The program provides the opportunity to gain exposure to multiple functional areas of the business. Called BLAST Analysts, participants rotate into a new assignment every six months. Between rotations, they participate actively in management, communication, store operations, and distribution center training as well as in the 360-degree feedback and mentor programs. Upon successful completion of the BLAST program, BLAST Analysts are given the opportunity to pursue positions of greater responsibility and accountability within the Blockbuster organization.

- Domino's, the pizza delivery company, has developed diversity awareness education classes to provide team members an opportunity, in a safe environment, to look at and discuss sensitive issues while giving them tools for handling those issues. Organizers create thought-provoking yet fun learning opportunities. Domino's has extended this opportunity through a new, online diversity training option for its general managers and assistant managers.

- Fairmont Hotels has set up an orientation program for its employees tailored around what it's like to be a guest. New employees may wear bathing suits during orientation to experience hot mineral baths and the spa. They could be treated to a penthouse champagne toast, have their cars valet-parked, or receive vouchers for a free night's stay.

- Walt Disney Parks and Resorts embodies the "hire for attitude, train for skill" axiom. For example, park sweepers are hired for their personality and then trained how to read body language so they can offer assistance to patrons before it's ever requested. It offers additional training on child abuse prevention. Disney bases its training on the belief that a park sweeper has among the highest number of guest contacts and is therefore a "key driver in guest satisfaction."

- Budget Rent-a-Car trains its counter staff at nearly 1,000 U.S. rental sites on company policies, problem solving, and customer satisfaction issues via interactive training. Around the country, instructors communicate with classes of up to seven students, who split into teams to act out hypothetical customer service and sales scenarios. Audio and data-based distance learning has decreased the overall training cost from $2,000 per student to only $156 per student. Through this interactive training, Budget is able to train a high percentage of new counter staff who can't fly to a training center due to family commitments or other personal constraints.

- Quarterly Sunday-morning meetings, nicknamed "Breakfast with Bernie and Arthur" (after Chairman Bernard Marcus and President Arthur Blank), are held for Home Depot's 23,000 employees. All employees are paid to attend the 45-minute program broadcast via satellite, in which company performance, growth plans, and a question/answer segment are presented.

- Pacific Coast Restaurants (PCR) provides one of the most intensive training and development programs in the industry with four-hour interactive employee orientations that get other employees involved. PCR realizes the importance of having a trainer, preferably a peer, sit in on the orientation to foster peer-to-peer connections. At the orientation, welcome gifts, which are unique to the department in which an employee is hired, are presented. Before the first day on the job, the assigned trainer treats the new employee to a meal and personally introduces them to coworkers. The trainer makes of point of publicly recognizing the employee's previous accomplishments and/or positions.

- Cultural diversity proved to be a stumbling block for Bob Chinn's Crab-House in Wheeling, Illinois, where about half of the employees don't speak English fluently. Most work as cooks, food preparation staff, dishwashers, and busboys in the restaurant's kitchen area. The vast majority of these workers are immigrants from Mexico and Central America. Managers discovered that the nationwide Welfare to Work Partnership had money available through Chicago Bizlink for training workers to improve work/life skills. They saw that the money could be used to establish in-house, English-speaking training programs. Officials with Bizlink were so impressed by the success of the ESL program at this venue that they decided to sponsor a class to help kitchen workers obtain their sanitation certifications from the health department.

- Denver-based Chipotle has been particularly aggressive in its ESL initiatives, because 75 percent of its workforce is Hispanic. Throughout the country, Chipotle's Culture, Diversity, and Language Program offers classes taught by store managers. The training, called "Walking a Mile in their Zapatas," also includes cultural training for managers and employees. The class, designed for beginners, runs for 60 to 90 minutes for 4 to 6 weeks, and employees are paid to attend. Its curriculum centers on "occupational" Spanish, which includes basic words and phrases needed in the workplace. Lessons cover practical topics such as answering the phone or communicating about numbers and money. Chipotle also contracts with outside institutions to teach 16-hour courses on "command" Spanish to non-Hispanic employees.

- Wells Fargo in Orange County, California, has created a Personal Banker Forward Hire Program that takes young bankers-to-be through an intensive, seven-week program combining classroom instruction with personal mentorship. Graduates of the program

are assigned to begin at a branch near where they live or plan to
live to begin their job as a personal banker.

- College students can find an avenue to a store management career through Wal-Mart's First In Line hands-on management
  training program. It's designed for associates who are currently attending college and have been with Wal-Mart for at least 90 days.
  Associates eligible to enroll in this program are those entering a
  four-year college or university and maintaining a course load of at
  least 12 hours with a 3.0 cumulative GPA. They also must show the
  desire and qualifications to get promoted within the company.

- Young people who join Enterprise Rent-A-Car say it's like getting
  an "MBA without the IOU." Enterprise seems to embody the, "Start
  at the bottom; work your way to the top," philosophy. Beginning
  as management trainees, employees soon find out they've been
  hired eventually to run their own business. After completing initial orientation and training, a trainee is assigned to a branch
  office in their home area to begin hands-on training. Because nearly
  100 percent of all managers and corporate executives started out
  as management trainees, knowledgeable mentors who once walked
  in their shoes teach the employees. Enterprise has implemented
  the following managerial career track for its rental operations:

  management trainee → assistant manager → branch manager
  → area manager → regional/group manager → VP/general
  manager

RETENTION

Leading employers know an impending labor shortage lurks around
the corner and have put employee retention strategies into practice with
ideas like these:

- Not only are employees eligible for a free or discounted meal
  when they work at McDonald's, but innovative programs are offered to each employee. Mc$ave, a prime reserve fund, helps em-
  ployees save money regularly; McDirect Shares, a direct stock
  purchase plan, builds employee ownership in McDonald's and allows them to reinvest dividends in the company; credit union
  membership makes it easy for employees to do their banking. All
  employees are eligible to attend Hamburger University, McDon-

ald's worldwide management training center in Oakbrook, Illinois, from which 65,000 McDonald's managers have graduated.

- In 1986, a group of Domino's Pizza franchisees formed The Partners Foundation, a nonprofit organization that assists team members in times of special need or after tragedies from natural disasters, unexpected afflictions, on-the-job accidents, and other emergencies. Since its inception, The Partners Foundation has helped thousands of Domino's Pizza team members and their families with financial, emotional, intermediary, and advisory assistance.

- Starbucks, the Seattle-based coffee empire, boasts an extremely low turnover rate for its industry, partly because it offers full-time and part-time employees not only a free pound of coffee each week but health benefits and stock options. All new partners go through an extensive orientation and fundamental training program to provide a solid foundation for career advancement at Starbucks. Educational programs include a course on the Starbucks passion for coffee that teaches understanding of its core product; a three-level program for baristas called Learning to Lead, which develops leadership skills, including store operation and effective management training; and the Starbucks Support Center (SSC), which offers classes ranging from basic computer skills to conflict resolution to management training.

- At Walt Disney Parks and Resorts, executives are required to sell popcorn, bus tables, stir fudge, and stock shelves during peak holiday periods. This cross-utilization program allows front-line employees to see that their work is valued, and it affords the leadership team an opportunity to understand the essence of the business.

- Muvico movie theater company has reduced turnover by 20 percent over a two-year period, resulting in a savings of approximately $1.2 million in both hard and soft costs. How? By implementing the correct "employment brand" along with its applicant screening process. Muvico identifies employees who are the "right fit," then trains them for success and continues to reward them for doing a great job.

- Available in every Whole Foods store are salary books that reveal gross salary statistics on each employee for the previous year. Whole Foods management believes that extreme differences in pay between front-liners and executives are detrimental, so it limits executive pay to 14 times that of its front-line employees and offers biweekly profit sharing based on work team productivity. This concept strongly emphasizes teamwork, which is also reflected by employees being involved in the hiring process.

- Dan Cathy, president and CEO of Chick-Fil-A, exemplifies "lead by example." Not only will you find him working behind the counter at least one day a year, just like the other 494 corporate employees, but he cooks and serves dinner to new franchise operators at his home—and even clears the dishes. Cathy also camps out with customers awaiting grand openings of Chick-Fil-A restaurants, where the first 100 customers win free chicken sandwich meals for a year.

- At Pizza Hut, it's all about the culture and how people are treated. These philosophies are reiterated continually, and 30 percent of the overall performance scorecard measures team member turnover. Pizza Hut has developed High Impact Coaching, a way to give feedback, talk to team members, and approach issues big and small.

- More than one-third of Pacific Coast Restaurants' management members began their PCR careers as servers and cooks. Individuals selected for promotion through the Kitchen Expert program or Front of the House Superstars program must pass a scrutinizing survey of their peers. All Career Progression candidates require coworker support to be accepted. Once approved, candidates spend 15 hours a week learning the administrative duties for their chosen pathways in addition to performing their normal functions as a server or cook. This training prepares them for a successful future as a full-time manager or sous-chef at one of the restaurants.

RECOGNITION

When coworkers at a small business commented on the benefits of a recognition program, one employee stated, "The only recognition people get around here is when the company president sees them at the holiday party and says, 'I recognize you from last year.'"

In *Quality is Free*, Phillip B. Crosby wrote, "Genuine recognition of performance is something people really appreciate. People really don't work for money. They go to work for it, but once the salary has been established, their concern is appreciation. Recognize their contribution publicly and noisily, but don't demean them by applying a price tag to everything."

A number of companies around the country have witnessed decreased turnover, enhanced productivity, and increased employee buy in as a result of various recognition programs and incentive plans they've implemented. Here's what some are doing.

- Even though KeySpan Corporation, the nation's fifth largest distributor of natural gas, employs more than 10,000 people, CEO Bob Catell routinely places personal calls to front-line employees to tell them they are doing a great job. If that person is unavailable, Catell will leave them a very personalized voice mail message, letting the front-liner know that they are one of the company's unsung heroes.
- The Service Fanatic Program at Muvico is an on-the-spot recognition program for exceeding service expectations, both internally and externally. Employees are given a Fanatic Card as a reward for good service, and for each five cards they receive, they're awarded a recognition pin to wear on their uniforms. Once a month, all Fanatic cards are placed into a drawing for prizes. When an employee has earned 25 cards, they get a $25 bonus and a plaque of recognition for achieving 5-Star Fanatic level.
- Auraria Library at the University of Colorado has instituted the elusive "day off" for faculty and support staff who have reached a milestone of service—5, 10, or 15 years. Awards are given for outstanding librarianship ($1,500), outstanding service ($500), and outstanding research/creative activity ($500). The recipients' dossiers are then forwarded to the university administration for consideration in university-wide awards.
- Most Blockbuster kidployees get perks such as flexible work schedules, paid sick and vacation days, tuition assistance, discount programs, and free movies and game rentals.
- Lowe's, a nationwide lumber/hardware dealer, offers its employees a free lunch on their birthdays.
- At Yum! Brands, Inc., a parent company comprised of KFC, Pizza Hut, and Taco Bell, recognition wasn't always important. Now it's high on their list. Across the country, management believes that recognition is everybody's responsibility, so Yum! Brands implemented formal service awards and created CHAMPS, a recognition program based on its operations principles: Cleanliness, Hospitality, Accuracy, Maintenance, Product, and Speed. Any employee can present a CHAMPS card to any other employee when they observe positive performance. The card includes a sticker

the recipient wears and a space for a personal comment. Each week, restaurant managers draw a winner from the completed CHAMPS cards. The winner is awarded a Priceless Reward—anything from a pair of movie tickets to having the manager wash the employee's car in the parking lot.

- Busch Gardens adventure park in Tampa, Florida, rewards outstanding employee activities with a Pat on the Back award and a memo placed in their employment file. Employees who provide a guest with exceptional service are given a scratch card that can be exchanged for a number of valuable rewards.
- Home Depot, the home improvement chain, selects an employee of the month in each store. That person receives $100 and a special badge to wear, plus gets their name added to a plaque at the front of the store. In addition, an employee receives another $50 after collecting five merit badges.
- The renowned golden arches that represent McDonald's are replicated in pieces of jewelry and presented to outstanding employees. Employees also have access to BeyondWork, a free Internet discount program that offers resources and savings on recreational products and services. And employees receive special savings on Disney Club memberships and catalog merchandise.
- Described in its 36-page booklet on "Recognizing Excellence," the North Carolina Department of Environment and Natural Resources encourages its employees to participate in a nominally priced recognition idea titled the CandyGram. To recognize someone, the booklet suggests attaching a note to one of the following edible items.

Lifesavers candies	For someone who has been a real "lifesaver" for you by holding down two jobs at once
Strawberry jam	For someone who has helped you out of a jam
100 Grand candy bar	For someone who has provided an invaluable service or saved the office some $$$$$
Nestles Crunch bar	For someone who was there for you at "crunch" time
Zero bar	For completing a tough project with zero errors
Three Musketeers bar	For the members of a great team

Mr. Goodbar	For anyone with a positive attitude that helps with office morale
Treat of recipient's choice	For someone who just needs a picker upper
Fireball	For someone who jumps right in and gets the job done without hesitation
York Peppermint Patty	For someone who has helped you out or is just especially invaluable: "They're worth a mint."
Snickers bar	For someone who keeps morale high with jokes and humor

- Genencor, a biotech company based in Palo Alto, California, believes in supporting an employee's entire lifestyle. Besides the normal benefits, Genencor offers free train and bus passes and signs out bikes and cars to employees who need to run errands during the business day.

- Kahala Corporation has $300 to $500 set aside each month for celebrating good days, bad days, good accomplishments, mistakes, and so on. Employees caught doing something right are recognized on the spot in front of the whole crew. Often, they're paid $5 to $20. Ideas are not only welcomed but also compensated with a bonus. The employee is asked to champion the idea and implement it. Employees respect ideas coming from their peers and try to come up with ideas themselves.

A

Advancement, 101–2
Air Force, U.S., 177
Alarm systems, 131
Alessandra, Tony, 19
Andy Griffith Show, The, 37–39
Antitheft devices, 131
Anxiety, 14
Appearances, 123–24. *See also* Dress
    code
Application procedure, 55–57
Army, U.S., 173–78
    appeal to core values, 174
    community and, 175–76
    excitement of, 176–77
    full disclosure and, 174–75
    ideas to borrow from, 177–78
Assessment tools, 46
    reducing turnover, 65–66
Atmosphere, workplace, 47–48,
    89–91
Attention deficit disorder (A.D.D.),
    14
Attitudes, of youth today, 10–11, 18
Auraria Library (University of
    Colorado), 195

B

Baby Boomers, 6
Background checks, 130
Bankruptcy, 128
Barnes & Noble, 47, 48
Behavior, 21, 119
Bias, 66
Blanchard, Ken, 80
Blank, Arthur, 190
Blockbuster, 189–90, 195
Bob Chinn's Crab-House, 191

Bonuses, 73
Border's Books, 48
Boredom, 89, 91
    cross training and, 183
Boys and Girls Clubs of America,
    188–89
Boyte, Phil, 143–44
Bread-and-butter (B&B) employees,
    29
Brooks, Herb, 43
Brother Leo, 142–43
Budget Rent-a-Car, 190
Burger King, 187
Busch Gardens, 196

C

Camaraderie, 178
CandyGram, 196–97
Cash, handling, 132
Cash register receipts, 132
Catell, Bob, 195
Cathy, Dan, 194
Cause and effect, 20
Cavin, Dennis, 174, 175
Challenge, 161, 170
CHAMPS, 195–96
Change, positive, 34
Character, judgment of, 66
Checks and balances system, 132
Chester, W. Grant, 5–6
Chester, Whitney, 78–79, 80
Chester, Zac, 23
Chicago Bizlink, 191
Chick-Fil-A, 194
Chipotle, 55–57, 191
Choice and consequence, 20
Chuck E. Cheese's, 165
Clarity, 119
Coaches, referrals from, 54

Coaching, 150–52, 163
Cold Stone Creamery, 159–65
Communication, 117–27, 141–42
 answering questions, 114
 employee theft and, 131–32,
  133–34
 Pal's Sudden Service and, 184
 rules/policies/procedures and,
  118–21
 service training and, 152
Company loyalty, 15, 96
Company values, 57
Compensation, 68–77, 99
 creative, 72
 demonstration of mastery and,
  104–5
 Eddie Bauer case study,
  73–74
 Enterprise case study, 74–76
 honesty and, 134
 incentives, 69, 73, 77
 lack of complaints and, 72
 longevity *vs.* performance,
  70–71
 minimum daily requirement
  and, 69–70
 offering better-than-average,
  103–5
 plan evaluation, 77
 Platinum Rule and, 72–73
 promotions tied to, 71–72
 retroactive raises, 104–5
 reward for exceeding
  production quotas, 70
 "team store initiative," 74
 vested interest, 69
Complaints, 72
Conflict resolution, 124–27
Conflicts
 dress code, 22–23
 lack of respect, 22
Cost of living, 103
Courtesy, 41
Cracker Barrel, 102–3
Creative outlets, 98
Crosby, Phillip B., 194
Crosby, Thom, 180, 181, 184
Cross training, 182–83

Customer service, 9, 57, 146–55
 coaching and, 150–52, 151–52
 employee empowerment and,
  152–53
 exposing employees to, 148–49
 model/mentor/motivate system,
  154–55
 Nordstrom and, 148
 reinforcing importance of, 155
 rewarding service excellence,
  153–54
 role-playing and, 150–51
 training and, 147–52

D

Damon, Matt, 94
Decotiis, Tom, 66
Decotiis Erhard, 66
Dick's Sporting Goods, 47, 48
Digital thinking, 19–21
Discipline, 122–23, 126
Disenfranchised employees, 28–29
Disgruntled employees, 6, 26–27
Domino's Pizza, 46–47, 190, 193
Dreamcatchers, 98
Dress code, 22–23, 123–24
Drug use, 14

E

Eddie Bauer, 72, 73–74
Edward D. Jones, 171
Elitch Gardens, 153
Empathy, 161
Employee(s)
 see also Recruitment/hiring
  strategies; Retention
 attitudes of "kidployee," 10–11
 bread-and-butter (B&B), 29
 disenfranchised, 28–29
 disgruntled, 6, 26–27
 finding ideal, 42–48
 foreign-born, 16
 gems, 30
 ideal, 37–41
 sabotage, 27
 solid subordinates, 29–30

theft and, 128–30. *See also*
    Honesty
total buy in, 30
Employee of the Month programs, 84
Employment laws, 45
Empowerment, 152–53, 160, 184–85
Enterprise Rent-a-Car, 74–76, 192
Environment (workplace), 47–48,
    89–91
Excitement, 176–77
Eye contact, 41

F

Fairmont Hotels, 190
Fallon Worldwide, 98
Fast-food industry, 65, 104, 179–85,
    194. *See also* Restaurants
Feedback, 126
First day of work, 110–13
Flexibility, 97
Foreign-born employees, 15
Fox, Robert, 66
Free agent mentality, 25
Friends, giveaways to, 133

G

GAD ("give a damn") Continuum,
    28–30, 32–33, 57
Gallup survey, 63
Gamers/gaming, 23–24, 176–77
Gems, 30
Genencor, 197
General Electric, 82, 144–45
Generation Xers, 6
Golden Rule, 19
Good Will Hunting, 94
Goretex®, 144
Grammar, 41
Great Harvest Bread Company, 114
Guidance counselors, 54
Guilt, 13

H

Halo 2, 23
Handshakes, 41

Hawthorne Plant experiments, 90
Heffel, Jerry, 170
Herman, Roger, 95–96
Hilton Hotels, 154
Hiring. *See* Recruitment/hiring
    strategies
Home Depot, 190, 196
Honesty, 41, 128–36, 169–70, 177
    clarification of rules, 131–32
    elimination of temptation and,
        132–33
    fair treatment and, 133–34
    screening job applicants, 130
    security systems and, 130–31
    setting an example, 134–36
Howard, Ron, 37
Hymowitz, Kay, 13
Hyperactivity, 14

I

Ice cream vendors, 159–65
Ikea, 189
Image, 22–23, 31, 97, 123–24
Immigrants, 15
Incentive, 69, 73, 77, 162–63
Inspiration, 34
Instant gratification, 14
Internet chat rooms, 141
Interviews, 66
Inventory inspections, 131

J–K

Jefferson Community College and
    Technical College, 189
Jostens, 53–54
Kahala Corporation, 188, 197
KeySpan Corporation, 195
KFC, 195

L

Leadership, 170–71
Liberation's Children (Hymowitz), 13
Link Crew®, 144
Longevity, 70–71
Long-term success, 32

Lowe's, 195
Loyalty, to company, 15, 96, 177

M

McDonald's Corporation, 104,
192–93, 196
MacKay 66, 139–40
MacKay, Harvey, 139–40
MacKay Envelope Company, 139
Malcolm Baldrige Award, 179
Management
employee turnover and, 105
impassioned, 138–39. *See also*
Mentorship
old-school, 18
shifts in attitudes and beliefs
and, 19
style, 88–94
Maney, Kevin, 23
Marcus, Bernard, 190
Marines, U.S., 177
Materialism, 6, 11, 12
Medication, 14
Mentorship, 137–45
character/passion and, 138–39
communication and, 141–42
company examples of, 144–45
connecting points, 139–41
freshman-senior link, 143–44
link to solid subordinate, 145
model behavior and, 142–43
Pal's Sudden Service and, 185
Merrill Lynch, 171
Metropolitan College, 189
Military enlistment, 173–78
MindData Systems, 66
Miracle, 43
Mistakes, 114
Modesty, 41
Monarch Ski & Snowboard Area, 187
Morale, 66
Motivation, 141
Muvico movie theater company, 193

N

National Institute of Media and
Family, 176

Navy, U.S., 177
Nordstrom, 148
North Carolina Department of
Environment and Natural
Resources, 196
"No soup for you," 11

O

One Minute Manager, The
(Blanchard), 80
Online shopping, 154
Open The Front Door Now formula,
125–27
Opie ideal, 37–41
Opportunity, 101–2, 161, 171
Orientation, 111–13
OTFDN. *See* Open The Front Door
Now formula
Outcome, varying, 92–93
Outrageous behavior, 21
Overmedication, 14

P

Pacific Coast Restaurants, 191, 194
Pagoda principle, 3–7
Pal's Sudden Service, 179–85
communication and, 184
cross training and, 182–83
employee empowerment and,
184–85
mentorship and, 185
perception of employees,
181–82
structure and, 182
Parental time, 13
Patrick, Craig, 43
Personality traits, 46, 66
Personal vested interest, 31
PetsMart, 188
Pizza Hut, 194, 195
Platinum rule, 19
Positive reinforcement, 79–80
Predictability, 90–94
Prescription drug use, 14
Pressure, 14
Problems, expressing, 133–34
Procedures, varying, 91–92

Production quotas, 70
Productivity, 177
Profiling, 44–47
Profits, 31
Promotions, 101–2
Prudential, 171

Q

Quality is Free, 194
Quality of life, 14
Qubein, Nido, 114

R

Rebellion, 21
Recognition, 78–87, 162–63, 171–72,
    194–97
    in all areas, 82–83
    cost of, 83
    perceived value of, 80–81, 94
    personal, 80–81
    pitfalls and traps, 83–84
    positive reinforcement, 79–80
    prompt/proportionate, 81
    public, 81–82
    showing appreciation, 98–100
    Sumner Regional Health
        Systems case study, 84–87
    varying rewards, 93–94
Recruitment/hiring strategies,
    49–57, 187–89
    application procedure, 55–57
    continuous, 50
    costs of, 64
    determining type of employee
        needed, 52–53
    follow-up, 57
    hiring decisions, 63
    key alliances and, 54–55
    methods, 51
    U.S. Army and, 173–78
Reference book sales, 166–72
Relationship building, 112, 178
Respect, 22, 41
Restaurants, 104, 114, 159–65, 188,
    194, 195–96
    Bob Chinn's Crab-House, 191
    Burger King, 187
    Chipotle, 55–57, 191
    Cracker Barrel, 102–3
    Domino's Pizza, 46–47, 190, 193
    McDonald's, 104, 192–93, 196
    Pacific Coast Restaurants, 191
    Pal's Sudden Service, 179–85
    Taco Bell, 188–89, 195
    White Castle, 104–5
Retailing
    Nordstrom, 148
    turnover and, 65
    Wal-Mart, 187, 192
Retention, 61–67, 192–94
    compensation and, 103–5
    Cracker Barrel case study,
        102–3
    improved working conditions,
        97–98
    intangibles, 64–65
    judging character and, 66
    ongoing process of, 105–6
    opportunity for advancement
        and, 101–2
    parents of employees and, 101
    providing support, 100–101
    showing appreciation and,
        98–100
    training and, 163–64
    turnover disruption and cost,
        62–66
Reverse discipline, 122–23
Rewards. *See* Recognition
Ritz Carlton hotel chain, 152–53
RoboStaff, 146–47
Rock Bottom Brewery, 46
Role playing, 150–51
Round Table Pizza, 114
Routine, 89
Rules
    be likable, 121
    consistency and, 120
    dress codes/appearance and,
        123–24
    enforcement of, 120–21
    fairness of, 119
    fun element and, 122
    relevancy of, 119–20
    resolving conflict, 124–27
    reverse discipline and, 122–23

S

Sabotage/saboteurs, 27, 28
Scheduling, 97
SEI Investments, 144
Self-actualization, 6
Self-esteem, 11–12
Self-expression, 21–23
    image, 22–23, 31, 97, 123–24
Sensory stimulation, 90
Service, community, 177
Service agreements, 134–35
Service economy, 8–9
Service Fanatic Program (Muvico),
    195
Simon Says, 137
Skills assessment, 112–13
Smiling, 41
Smith, Douglas, 174
Snowbird Ski Area, 51
Solid subordinates, 29–30
Southwestern Company, The, 166–72
    character building, 168–69
    job requirements, 167–68
    principles and values of, 169–72
Speaking quality, 41
Spiderman 2, 23
"Spikes" program, 85–86
Spiritualism, 13
Standards, 119
Starbucks, 193
Stimulation, 177
Students in Free Enterprise (SIFE),
    187
Studer, Quint, 85
Studer Group, The, 85
Success, long-term, 32
Sumner Regional Health Systems,
    84–87
Swim with the Sharks (McKay), 139

T

Taco Bell, 188–89, 195
Talent, recognizing, 34
Tax considerations, 64
Teachers, referrals and, 54
Team store initiative compensation
    plan, 74

Teamwork, 163, 178
TEENSupreme program, 188–89
Temptation, eliminating, 132–33
Theft, employee, 128–30. *See also*
    Honesty
Time, *vs.* money, 13
Tokyo Joes, 51
Total buy in, 27, 30, 34
Trader Joe's, 187
Training, 160–61, 163–64
    cross training, 182–83
    customer service and, 147–52
    entertainment and, 115–16
    showing relevance/benefits of,
        115
    updating materials, 113–14
Tuition reimbursement programs, 104
Turnover, 62–63, 95–96
    see also Retention
    reasons for, 96
    as socially pervasive problem, 67
    tests/assessments and, 65–66

U

Unemployment claims, 64
United Parcel Service (UPS) School
    to Work program, 189
University of Louisville, 189
Us/Them, Then/Now quadrant,
    9–10, 16

V

Values, 18, 57
    U.S. Army and, 174
Vested interest, 31
Video games, 23–24
Video surveillance cameras, 131
Vocational teachers, 54
Volume Library, The, 166

W–Y

Wal-Mart, 187, 192
Walt Disney Parks and Resorts, 190,
    193
Welch, Jack, 82

Welfare to Work Partnership, 191
Wells Fargo, 188, 191–92
Westinghouse, 90
White Castle restaurants, 104–5
Whole Foods, 188, 193–94
Wieden+Kennedy, 188
W.L. Gore & Associates, 144
Work environment, 47–48, 89–91
    improving, to slow turnover,
        97–98

Work ethic, 5–7, 9–10
    free agent mentality, 25
    vs. self-esteem, 11–12
    shift away from traditional,
        24–25
    Us/Them, Then/Now quadrant
        and, 16
Work-life balance, 97
WOW cards, 83–84
Yum! Brands, Inc., 195

Eric Chester is the premier expert on Generation Why; in fact, he coined the term. Since 1986, Eric Chester has been speaking to and working with Generation Why youth. He has personally addressed more than two million teenagers and is dialed in to the mindset of this burgeoning generation. He frequently appears on national media (*Good Morning America,* MSNBC, *FoxNews,* CNN, *Canada AM,* etc.) to provide insight, perspective, and strategies for educating and employing post-Generation Xers.

The founder and CEO of Generation Why, Inc., Eric is in high demand as a keynote speaker and consultant by companies and organizations that rely heavily on 16-year-olds to 24-year-olds as their front-line employees. His clients include Toys "R" Us, Dairy Queen, Harley-Davidson, Arby's, Bell South, and Wells Fargo. His book *Employing Generation Why— Understanding, Managing, and Motivating Your New Workforce* (2002, Tucker House Books) is a must-read for business owners, managers, and executives.

Eric is a 2004 inductee into the International Speakers Hall of Fame, an honor shared by less than 2 percent of all professional speakers in the world. The proud father of two and stepfather of two, he lives in Colorado with his wife, Lori.

Eric can be reached by visiting **http://www.generationwhy.com.**